FATHERLY
Influence

A Man's Finest Legacy

For Rick,
Happy fathers day

Winston "Terry" Sutherland, PhD

All the best
Terry Sutherland 6/9/2013

WESTBOW
PRESS
A DIVISION OF THOMAS NELSON

WestBow Press books may be ordered through booksellers or by contacting:

WestBow Press
A Division of Thomas Nelson
1663 Liberty Drive
Bloomington, IN 47403
www.westbowpress.com
1-(866) 928-1240

ISBN: 978-1-4497-9581-8 (sc)
ISBN: 978-1-4497-9582-5 (e)

Library of Congress Control Number: 2013909262

Printed in the United States of America.

WestBow Press rev. date: 5/22/2013

Table of Contents

This book is dedicated to all men who are
determined to be positive fatherly mentors
and build fine legacies with their kids.

Preface

Fathers are the pride of their children. They are heroes and icons to their little boys and girls. Since the dawn of time, the patriarch has been firmly recognized as a child's grounding influence. Aware that bending a tree is possible when it is still young and pliable, not when it is old and brittle, mentoring dads cultivate in their young, the wisdom of skillful living. And because adults feed off their childhood experiences, dad's nurturing affects everything kids do lasting their whole lives through.

Fatherly Influence: A Man's Finest Legacy discusses the advantages a mentoring father embodies. It honors dads who are worthy of the hero status their kids ascribe to them. It harkened to the cry of countless children growing up without the affirmation and guidance of their fathers. It recognizes that every son and daughter yearns to, not only bask in the love and nurturing of a mother's love, but also to flourish in the protection and confidence a father imparts.

Because the greater need is often created by absentee or uninvolved fathers, this book focuses on the power of fatherly influence. It does not pretend to address every issue the ideal mentoring father may encounter; but it attempts to provide a thorough treatment. The goal is to be a voice in the important discussion of the influence father has on his offspring's happiness and success. Convinced that dads play a big part in shaping the identities of their children, it is hoped this candid discussion inspires dad to step into his most dignified role—creating a lasting legacy with his kids.

Impetus

Owing, in part, to that gut-feeling that something is missing, this subject has been of great personal interest. And although it wasn't always obvious, this curiosity shadowed every stage of my life's journey. Perhaps my lack of a fatherly mentor has been the greatest catalyst fueling this quest. It is probably the high price of my father's absence which gave birth to *Fatherly Influence*. If the adage, "Necessity is the mother of invention" holds true, then this may provide an explanation for the compelling hunger I felt for my own fatherly mentor.

So the contents developed within the confines of these pages emerged from a deep seated cry of the human spirit—one that not only fatherless boys and girls know, but also children of disengaged and cruel fathers are all too familiar with. As a result of this unrelenting inward call, I have sought out mentors for myself, explored the pros and cons of mentoring relationships, researched the topic of mentoring, and both volunteered for many years as a mentor and directed mentorship programs. These have strengthened my resolve to promote mentoring relationships across the entire spectrum of human experience. And because of the special place fathers hold in our lives, coupled with the dismal track record left by many deadbeat dads, *Fatherly Influence* was produced as a labor of love.

Many children long to experience a father's tender, masculine love; too many are being deprived of a natural male presence and perspective. The casualties, strewn along life's byways, foul the air with the stench of neglect and abandonment. Like the 800 Pacos of Spain, a father's role in his child's life may not be taken lightly. In this narrative, a Spanish son ran away from home because of a strained relationship with his dad. After months of searching, the father took out an Ad in their local newspaper. It read, "Dear

Paco, meet me in front of this newspaper's office on Saturday around noon. All is forgiven, I love you." To the father's surprise, when noontime on Saturday arrived, 800 Pacos showed up to be forgiven and loved by their fathers.

Having spoken with many who've never experienced fatherly affection, they're resigned to the notion that it is a deficit they will take with them to their graves. This sense of paternal abandonment is a constant companion to the fatherless who can only fantasize about what having a dad might be like. I'm convinced that if the above advertisement were to be published in say, New York, with "Dear Mike" instead of "Dear Paco," a larger crowd of broken boys is liable to flood the city. "Dear Jennifer" may attract more girls than either of them.

Approach

Two specific approaches have been used to facilitate this discussion. Firstly, I have tapped into my own experiences, my own longing for those things (not material) a good dad provides his children and the things I hope to provide mine. Secondly, because dad's rich influences are best observed from average, everyday, people, I have provided them opportunity to reflect upon their dads and their experiences raising their own kids; they then shared their thoughts in a questionnaire. As a result, some of the opinions and suggestions discussed herein naturally reflect my worldview, background, and upbringing. Other ideas came directly from the questionnaire, *Survey of Fatherly Influence*, which appears in the appendix. The survey was taken by participants at several area colleges, passengers of the New York City Subway System, pedestrians in Brooklyn, New York and Dallas, Texas, and range in age between 18 and 78. Many of the participants were parents although not all of them. Those who were not parents were still able to provide valuable insight because they had fathers and spoke of his influence in their lives. Even those who weren't raised by a father spoke to the issue from the perspective of a fatherless child.

May this labor of love be received with a sentiment commensurate to that with which it was conceived.

Winston Sutherland
Brooklyn, New York
May, 2013

Author's Note

atherly Influence: A Man's Finest Legacy is not so much a book on parenting as much as it is a candid chat about the power of fatherly mentoring. Chapter 2 is devoted to explaining the difference. Apart from God, no one can rightly tell another how to raise their children. And this book doesn't attempt to do so. Instead, this is a brief discussion for fathers to understand their enormous influence in their children's lives and to follow through by mentoring them. It is intended to be a clarion call for dads to "enjoy the ride" showing their offspring how to navigate successfully through life. I believe the best way to accomplish that is for "Pops" to see mentoring, not as a chore but as an opportunity to provide his young a head-start in the race of life. Kids are looking to dads for it.

Who Should Read This Book?

veryone. This is one of those books that everybody should read. Although the title and contents of *Fatherly Influence* focus on dad's influence in his children's lives, it is by no means a testosterone, macho, or alpha-male driven exercise in male chauvinism. On the contrary, wives, daughters, mothers, sons, and fathers can all appreciate the place and significance of a father's role in his kids' lives. The dearth of fatherly presence in the home is well documented. It is therefore encouraged that everyone read *Fatherly Influence* and encourage others to look into this important subject.

Chapter 1

More Than an ATM

My heroes are and were my parents.
I can't see having anyone else as my heroes.
—Michael Jordan

Monday Morning Stories

Timothy Banks, Jr. beamed with delight as he dramatized another weekend adventure with his dad. He became animated and fired-up when telling tales of their Saturday escapades. I found myself looking forward to his stories at the dawn of each new week. You couldn't wait to hear the next cool thing Timmy did with his dad or the exotic places they explored together. His excitement couldn't be contained in his tiny frame as his bright eyes, broad smile, and pumped fist betrayed his glee. Though this happened over thirty years ago, the memory is as fresh as if it were just yesterday. Timmy's thirteen-year old tenor voice pierced through the Monday morning grogginess with phrases like, "Man, we hiked up Bear Mountain following the trail of the river last Saturday. You've never seen any place like it. Man oh man, we went hunting; and daddy was telling us crazy stories about the things he did with his cousins when they were little. That man is crazy with a capital "K". You can't believe the things he can do. When we finally got up there, we played tag football..." And on, and on, and on, he went. Then he ended with, "my daddy is the best daddy in the whole world!" These are bits and pieces of the scenes still fresh in my memory from sitting on the fringes of that curious group hanging on his every word. A stranger walking in, unable to hear what was being said, might misinterpret that vein on his neck about to pop, the teardrop breaking away from his eye, and his high-pitched voice rambling on at 100 mph speeds. These weren't expressions of agony but of excitement and happiness. The chorus of giggles sprinkling the sleepy Brooklyn classroom confirmed the light-hearted mood created by the amateur storyteller. This became a regular Monday morning feature as classmates swapped weekend stories. If Timmy's adventures weren't enough, during recess he'd whip out a stack of money he got from his dad and he'd have his pick of the tastiest treats from school-yard vendors. Most of us, if we had any money at all, budgeted our few coins to negotiate the best snack we could afford. After school, Timmy's dad picked him up in his "supped-up" Maxima blasting "fresh" music and cruised off to their home.

Perhaps my physical location on the outskirts of that loyal congregation betrayed the apprehension I felt having no such stories to contribute. There was no way I could enter into such sacred territory without fabricating a tall tale; and believe me you'd be tempted to do so. But I could not relate to their experiences because my weekends were filled with family chores and the occasional backyard games with my brothers—we certainly didn't go anywhere. The only outings I could talk about were the yearly Sunday school picnic at a large park somewhere upstate New York, and an annual trip to Jones beach. And of course, the yearly week-long camp at some faraway place. And they were all wonderful; I looked forward to them every year. But the bigger reason I couldn't relate was that I knew very little about my father because he hadn't been around since I attained the incredibly mature age of two. There was no opportunity to do anything together with him. And you knew the floor was open to members only—you had to have a daddy who played with you to be a member. Needless to say, I didn't qualify.

Watching Junior High kids try to "one-up" each other for bragging rights over whose daddy was best can leave deep impressions on kids with "rolling-stone" dads.

Looking back, those scenes functioned like a giant stethoscope, listening attentively to the exciting pulse of a father's involvement—or perhaps that of a massive searchlight, exposing a previously unnoticed father absence. Those moments of innocent schoolboy chatter made me aware of my paternal need; they awoke in me awareness of my dad's absence. Prior to that, I had not missed him; I guess I didn't really think about him much until that point. And I had no idea fathers could be fun, friendly, or kind-hearted. It was only later on in life that the saying, "The glory of children are their fathers," took on special meaning for me. Being told that I was fortunate to escape his tyranny served only to exacerbate my ambivalence within. Back then, a father to me equated to being rough, demanding, and mean-spirited. There was no room in my idea of "father" for one who exhibited patience and understanding, let alone, fun. Those Monday morning stories, whether exaggerated or not, served as the launching pad of a subconscious quest for wholeness. This ultimately led to my personal resolution that, "If I ever have children of my own, not only would I never abandon them, but I would be sure to love them the way I would want my father to love me."

In some mysterious way, I get the feeling that if I live to be 110 years old I'd always yearn for the missing piece in the parental equation. It's one of those things that keeps eluding you, that keeps nibbling at your guts, that has you grasping at straws from time to time.

I realize that I was privileged to have the best possible mother anyone could ever hope for. We never lacked for food, clothing, shelter, and a strong sense of being loved. And even though it might have been easy (even tempting), she never attempted to badmouth our father to us. It is hard to imagine life without her infinite store of love, wisdom, and good humor. But walking around with chinks in my battle armor made vulnerable by my father's disappearance, unmasked at least two hidden needs. It exposed questions I didn't realize I had; and it ushered me into a complex world for which I found myself unprepared.

A big part of me wishes this was true of only a few isolated cases. But unfortunately, this brief autobiographical piece isn't uncommon; it is the experience of many. Naturally, the stories are unique to each individual's personal history, but millions of fatherless boys and girls live their entire lives with deficits created by the incomplete parental formula. And like me, many of them suspect that if they live to be 110, they will carry that internal vacuum with them to their graves. The good news is, going forward we can all blaze a different trail with our kids.

Experiences during our earliest years work like time-released pills—informing and affecting later behavior throughout our lifetimes. What was deposited by our guardians at that formative stage, we subconsciously return to time and time again. Even things which weren't part of our experiences but of which we knew something was missing tend to live in our imaginations and we dabble with the elusive question, what if, what if? Because of our resilient human spirit, many appear to be whole. But the courageous among us have acknowledged the missing ingredient in the parental recipe and have pledged to break the cycle by producing more complete little people better prepared for life. And many, like me, have resolved never to desert their kids but to love them the same way they would want to be loved by their fathers.

Providing children a secure family is one of the most loving and stabilizing things dads do. Any discussion of fatherly influence and the legacy dads may create naturally begins with the family.

Family's Privileged Position

Whoever said, "The strength of a nation lies in the homes of our people," understood the pivotal role the family plays in a viable society. Someone else put it into even stronger terms, "No nation could be destroyed while it possesses a good home life." As separate but related ideas, these words pay homage to the supremacy of a sound family unit. As the family goes, so goes the society. When this kinship unit is weak or divided, the nation is compromised and vulnerable; when the family is strong and unified, the society is fortified and robust.

But families the world over have been bombarded by every enemy known to man. From the ravages of drug abuse to the subtle erosion of family values, the family unit constantly fends off a flurry of foreign threats. Of course, anything of real value finds itself needing protection from a host of threats, thefts, and ill-advised alliances. And the family heads the list of precious things needing not only protection, but cultivation, nurturing, maintenance, and check-ups to retain its health and viability. Speaking at the 2012 Harlem Book Fair, Dr. Khalil Muhammad, director of the Schomburg Center for Research in Black Culture at the New York Public Library said, "Marriage is a declining institution in the world." Needless to say, since marriage is on the decline, then the family as we know it is also on the decline.

Made up of individual members, the family unit may be the epicenter of social development and provides for basic relationships: father, mother, husband, wife, brother, and sister. It is there, within the confines of the home, that we experience a microcosm of all that life has to offer. Like an apple seed which contains all the future characteristics of a big, sprawling, apple tree, all that a child may eventually become is bound up within the home. The average family member experiences both ups and downs, and good and bad; there is security and love, along with disappointments and correction. A thriving family shares responsibilities so that no one becomes overburdened and children learn how to work in teams, contributing to their overall wellbeing. It is in the home that we learn how to share with others, how to relate to authority, and the important little things like how not to speak out-of-turn. There our value-system is shaped; we develop our sense of right and wrong—the conscience is trained. Within the secure environment, we feel safe to drop our guards and expose our true personalities. There is no need for pretenses, no image to uphold—members feel free to be themselves. For many, home is the place they feel most comfortable, peaceful, and at rest—hence the saying to "feel at-home." This may account for the reason home holds the potential for the greatest amount of joy and frighteningly the greatest amount of pain. The task of providing a stable and balanced environment which ultimately determines the plight of the nation lies within the home—the parents shouldering the greater responsibility, the father embracing a leading role.

The Parental Privilege

Both parents are entrusted with this noble honor. It has been dubbed the toughest job on the planet. Some have referred to it as a thankless job. Which parent will dispute that it requires a full-time commitment? The parental role taps resources of time, energy, money, moral fiber, and emotional fortitude. It involves a partnership between mother and father to nurture their children in every facet of their lives. Good ones pay attention to the whole person, the physical, emotional, spiritual, social, and educational complexities all colliding within each individual child.

An ancient document contains a telling statement which, too often has not been given its proper due; the idea is that, "a man should leave his mother and father and cling to his wife." These familiar words are rightly thought of in the context of marriage. They underscore the importance of a man's independence from his parents and his commitment to his new wife. It may even suggest that his energies ought to be directed to building his own home. But what some seem to miss is the implication directed at parents. For, since there should come a time when a man leaves his mother and father (declaring his independence and manhood) to cling to his wife (taking on responsibility to start his own family), his parents are the ones to get him ready to do both. They must prepare him to navigate successfully through the twists and turns life will fling at him. Before young men and women leave home to be joined to their spouses, they are under the jurisdiction, guidance, and tutelage of their parents; and they ought to be well prepared before they are released in the world.

Home-leavers need to know how to provide for a family which requires learning a skill that will earn them a living. Learning how to interact socially with various people in society has always been important for all to master. The importance of networking has been known and practiced by the well-to-do for many years and is now common knowledge even among the working class. Many times, social etiquettes aren't taught in the classroom. Parents must pass-on those critically important skills. It was world heavyweight boxing champion Muhammad Ali who seemed to be keenly aware of this when he said, "Friendship… is not something you learn in school. But if you haven't learned the meaning of friendship, you really haven't learned anything." Here is a successful icon emphasizing the importance of mastering certain subtle social skills they don't teach in school but which have the potential to either make or break us. There are appropriate ways to relate to the opposite sex; those acceptable codes of conduct may be passed on by parents. The young adult ought to know how to respect the law and people in authority and how to best get along with their fellowmen. They should know how to think critically and not merely react emotionally to new or opposing ideas. When Junior and Princess finally pack up their belongings and leave home, they should be prepared for life. They should inherit their family-brand cell phone with their personalized "Apps for success" to start their own families? Of course, they won't know everything; but, it would be helpful if they had certain fundamentals young adults ready to leave home should have. They should at least have their parents' philosophy and their life-formula as a resource and guide. These "Apps for success" are passed on through a process of mentoring.

So, it is important that parents fully appreciate the privilege they have inherited. No one can put a price on the gift of steering another human being to maturity. And as it is with anything of great privilege, it is a package deal coupled with equally great responsibility. Ask any successful parent, they'll readily admit that the sacrifice and toil invested in parenthood yield untold rewards. To them, the satisfaction and joy they get from raising Princess and Junior is worth some sleepless nights, stress, and hard work.

Morrie Schwartz comes to mind as an excellent example of such a father. He was introduced to us in 1995 by ABC-TV's *Nightline*, featuring anchorman Ted Koppel, and later in 1997 through the bestselling book, *Tuesdays with Morrie*, written by his student Mitch Albom. Morrie was interviewed on *Nightline* because their producers were enamored with his courage to stare down death's corridors while dispensing life-lessons to anyone who'd listen. One Tuesday, while meeting with his mentor/professor during the final months of his life, Mitch recorded his conversation with Morrie.

> "Whenever people ask me about having children or not having children, I never tell them what to do," Morrie said… "I simply say, 'There is no experience like having children.' That's all. There is no substitute for it… If you want the experience of having complete responsibility for another human being, and to learn how to love and bond in the deepest way, then you should have children."
>
> So you would do it again? I asked…

"Would I do it again?" he said to me, looking
surprised. "Mitch, I would not have missed the
experience for anything. Even though..."
"Even though there is a painful price to pay,"
he said... "Because I'll be leaving them *soon*"
(Albom, 1997, p.93).

The paternal privilege is not only rewarding to both father and
child, it is also very gratifying to dads. Naturally, the fathers who
get the most out of this experience are the ones who approach
fatherhood with a focus on its privilege—not as a burden to
bear. It's all in the attitude, the mindset, and the perspective.
The rearing of children anywhere involves things common
across cultures: providing food, clothing, and security; teaching
values and attitudes; modeling beliefs and behaviors; correcting,
encouraging, working, playing, laughing, and crying; dealing with
bad times and good times, and so on. These are the constants;
every family deals with these in their own way, these don't change.
But what changes are the parents in charge of managing them.
What's different is how a parent approaches them. A parent may
approach his fathering role in one of two ways: as a long, thorny,
clock-watching, 18-21 years of forced labor or as an opportunity
he's salivating for—where he prepares his young to grab life by
the horns and live it to its fullest. It all depends on the perspective
dad takes. If he takes the first option, viewing fatherhood as
begrudging years of forced labor, both dad and child will find
those years to be a grind, like doing hard time, tiresome, even
tedious; but if the second option is pursued, where he's eager to
steer his kids to an abundant life, both father and child have a
much better chance for a lifelong adventure of happily building
something special together. I vote for the second option and I'm

Winston "Terry" Sutherland, PhD

not alone. Eighty-seven percent of the participants in the *Survey of Fatherly Influence* believe that successful parents provide much more than the basics of food, clothing, and shelter; they ready their kids to face the world. They nurture, coach, and mentor them to the threshold of adulthood.

Dad Is More Than An ATM

The father's role in this may not be belittled; his unique contribution to his children's life-readiness is particularly needed. Unfortunately, we as men have fumbled the ball when it comes to mentoring our kids. And it shows in the attitudes and behaviors displayed in our sons and daughters. It was said that the largest number of collect calls were made on Father's day. How telling. Many dads' total fathering effort amounts to footing the bill for items of clothing, schoolbooks, and the odd birthday gift for their little girl or boy. Others must pay child support fees; and some, only because they're obligated to do so. Quite a few go further into their wallets, so much so, that when Princess or Junior needs anything, daddy suddenly comes to mind; other than that he's a forgotten man. But dad is more than an ATM. He's not merely an automatic teller machine dispensing cash upon demand. He isn't only useful when kids need things. Sure, one of his main roles is that of provider but it's only *one* of his roles. He also protects, influences, coaches, guides, comforts, assures, advises, and does much more. Great dads enrich the whole person. They raise their children, teaching them how to do life. By the way, it is this puzzle that children are looking to their fathers to solve—the puzzle of life, how to do life? How to live skillfully? How to interpret this complex, sometimes elusive, and fragile minefield of life? Although they don't realize it, kids are looking for a tried and true path. Not unlike the father who took his son rock-climbing, while on a tricky spot on the mound, the son yelled out to his father "Choose the good path dad I'm following right behind you." In more ways than one, that's exactly what children are saying to their dads—choose the good path because we're looking to you for direction.

We have our poets to thank for their ability to express our deepest feelings in beautiful prose. They have mastered the art of capturing life's moments in the most artistic manner. Here are a few lines which seem to capture the unspoken power of our influence upon our young.

> There are little hands all eager
> To do everything you do;
> and a little boy who's dreaming
> Of the day he'll be like you.
> —Author Unknown

Because of the value of these precious little souls residing within our homes, fathers can ill-afford to treat their privilege lightly. Not only shouldn't he be reduced to a portable bank but he also shouldn't be limited to making deposits to the sperm bank. He's not a mere sperm donor either. He's more than a sperm donor too. Children are people, real human beings with body, soul, and spirit. They deserve the very best from us. They deserve to be loved and respected. Sure they're little, but they are no less full and complete persons. Remember, we were once little too and we hated the times we felt neglected. They may be undeveloped but all the parts are there. Fathers ought to be careful not to treat them with any less value because of their temporarily tiny stature. We get to develop them in all their components—body, soul, and

Winston "Terry" Sutherland, PhD

spirit. And they are totally dependent upon us for physical, social, and spiritual development, protection, love, and guidance. How unfortunate it would be to reduce dad to a mere "sugar-daddy" of an ATM.

Why Mentor?

To underscore the value of selecting an effective approach to the patriarchal task, we need only look to the most pragmatic segment of our society which cares only for the bottom line— dollars and cents. Corporate America wastes little time with techniques and methods which fail to produce desired results. They spend incredible amounts of resources to identify and sharpen the tools which maximize their profits. So when it comes to readying their talented staff for optimum success, they turn to the most effective method, mentoring. This involves an experienced professional coaching a novice with the intention of readying her for a particular mission. Corporate giants and community organizers pledge by this time-honored method of transferring traditions and company know-how during an extended period of apprenticeship. Researcher Dave Thomas (2001) of Harvard University conducted a study of mentoring practices at three firms: a high-tech firm, a manufacturer, and an electronics firm. His results showed that, "Successful people of color who advanced the furthest had a strong network of mentors and sponsors who nurtured their professional development." The world of sport is replete with scenarios which mimic real life issues. Take, for instance, a story reported at the games of the 20th Olympiad by the coach of arguably the greatest Olympian of all time, Michael Phelps. During an interview about the record breaking swimming athlete, Bob

Bowman reported that as coach he had to help Phelps prepare for the unexpected. One time he had Phelps fill his goggles with water and place it over his eyes while he swam competitively by counting arm strokes until he touched the wall. Sure enough, in 2008 during a competitive race, his goggles somehow filled up with water and totally blurred his vision. But because he was well mentored, he did not panic. He was able to relax and concentrate on completing his race by counting arm-lengths to the end of the race just like he practiced. The result? Another gold medal! Mentoring results like these may be seen across virtually every facet of life. When the top performers in the world, be they fortune 500 companies or the best athletes we have ever produced, want to be successful, they choose to mentor.

If the need for fathers to mentor their children seems somehow optional and less than a priority, the evidence on the effects of fatherless children may present additional food for thought. The collective voice of research is unanimous on the issue of dad's absence from the home. A 1999 US D.H.H.S news release reported that, "Fatherless boys and girls are: twice as likely to drop out of high school; twice as likely to end up in jail; and four times more likely to need help for emotional or behavioral problems" (March 26, 1999). More recently, January 2012, the Children's Defense Fund reported on the state of children in New York. These were some of their findings: Number of...

Children who are victims of neglect & abuse	77, 011
Children in foster care	26, 783
Children adopted from foster care	2, 205
Grandparents raising grandchildren	131, 108

As the foundation of society, the 21st century family unit is less than rock-solid. And although both parents are indispensible to their kids' success, the father in particular fashions a fine legacy when providing loving leadership, affirming their identity, being present, being involved, and being an example.

We have always benefitted from observing the behavior of various creatures in the animal kingdom. Mockingbirds are faced with an interesting choice when they find their young in captivity. It is said that a mother or father bird will seek out and find its young which have been captured and caged. With distances extending as far as a mile from their nesting place, mockingbirds will pursue their young, and when they find them they feed them until they can care for themselves. These very social birds are easily domesticated but if the parent bird continues to see that their young aren't being released, they will make the tough decision to feed them poison berries. Ornithologists (bird experts) tell us that mockingbirds make the choice to die rather than to live in captivity. To mockingbirds, living in captivity is no way to live at all. They value their freedom too much to settle for a substandard life of bondage. Fathers, who mentor their young, value "the best possible life for their kids" too much to neglect their need for father guidance. To these fathers, being absent from their kids' lives is no way to live at all.

Sometimes the concern may not be fatherly absence but fatherly disengagement. Dad may be physically present but emotionally absent; he may be in-and-around the house but out-and-about mentally and socially. He may be uninvolved in his children's lives. And while there may be several reasons for this common occurrence, one surprising reason he's not actively mentoring Junior and Princess is that he simply may not know how. We tend to teach the way we were taught, love the way we were loved, mentor the way we were mentored. So if dad didn't particularly receive any real mentoring from his father, there is a strong likelihood he will not mentor his son or daughter either. Though this may be, it is no reason for him to comfort himself with the delusion, "I wasn't mentored and turned out fine, so there is no great consequence if I don't mentor Junior and Princess, they'll turn out fine too." Even if that statement contains a bit of truth, he'll probably be willing to admit that he would have done even better if his father mentored him. Also, things are more complicated nowadays. Things were simpler a generation or two ago. Not knowing how, does not absolve dad from his natural paternal calling to thoroughly coach Junior and Princess before ushering them into an increasingly complex world. What dad doesn't know, he can learn as he goes along.

Another reason some fathers aren't mentoring their young may be the perception that it isn't macho or manly to mentor. Some dads believe somewhere deep within them, that mentoring his son or daughter is better left to their mother. To these men, mentoring is too much like nurturing and men just don't nurture. That is too "touchy-feely," too sensitive—let the women handle that sort of thing, they're good at that! Of course, nothing could be further from the truth. Sure, they may or may not be good at it but they cannot do it all. Father's input is crucial to Princess and Junior's overall development.

Yet another reason some men don't mentor their children may result from a reaction to the overly controlling influence their own fathers may have had in their lives. Since their fathers had his hand in everything they did, producing in them the feeling of suffocation, they react to that unfortunate experience by going to the other extreme of adopting a hands-off, almost anything goes, approach to raising their kids.

Winston "Terry" Sutherland, PhD

Finally, kids want their fathers to mentor them. I know I did. And the majority of participants in the *Survey of Fatherly Influence* agreed that they would want their fathers to mentor them. Young people are yearning for a guide. They'd love to have a dad in whom to confide, go to for help when untangling life's web of confusing issues, and a trustworthy man by whom they can run half-baked ideas. Like a backbone to the human body, dad's contribution provides stability.

But whatever the reason one offers for not preparing his offspring to flourish in life, he must keep in mind that mother alone can't do it; father is needed to play his important part. He is more than an ATM; he is a natural influencer and mentor. Giving mentoring a chance, he'll enjoy creating his kid's Monday morning stories, entering them into the honored "proud child of daddy club," and he'll discover the joy of his finest legacy.

Chapter 2

Parenting Vs. Mentoring

Skillful living is a perishable art. It must be passed on as a personal skill. Otherwise it is lost.
—Adapted from Jascha Heifetz

Beyond The Basics

Before we delve into the important part father must play by unleashing his influential power, it may be helpful to address questions some are undoubtedly asking.

"What's the difference between parenting and mentoring? Aren't they essentially the same?" Is there enough of a difference between them to warrant a discussion?

Absolutely!

While mentoring and parenting go hand in hand, there are significant differences which can either empower our young on the road to intelligent, skillful, and happy living; or set them up for an unwise, frustrating, and miserable existence.

The label "Mentor" actually comes from Greek mythology—although, both the concept and its practical application have their place firmly rooted in the family. Mentor was a loyal friend and adviser to king Odysseus of Ithaca. When Odysseus was away at war, Mentor helped raise his son, Telemachus. Mentor became Telemachus' tutor, coach, counselor, and protector. With all that time spent together, these two eventually built a relationship based on affection and trust. This is not unlike the many nannies, maids, or domestics who care for children of the middleclass and wealthy in society. They tend to develop a bond with them, impacting their impressionable minds during the formative years. It is from this ancient relationship that the name mentor has been adopted and used to refer to individuals who perform that role of knowledgeable and experienced coach to a younger person. So, mentors are experienced tutors who provide guidance to a novice student with the hopes of readying him for a certain task. They take the naïve and help them arrive at a level of understanding and maturity. They help make the simpleminded sophisticated. The fatherly mentor steps into the role of experienced teacher to guide and coach his children driven by his natural paternal affection toward them.

To be sure, parenting and mentoring are related. In fact, some have struggled to separate the two. When I was younger, my mom would warn, "Watch out for Slick; his hands are so quick he can steal milk out of coffee." The relationship between parenting and mentoring is so intricate that it may require the skill of Slick to dissect them. It is more like separating milk from coffee than say, separating apples from oranges. But although they share common interests, namely the preparing of their young for life, the roles of parenting and mentoring may not always be one and the same. Like coffee and milk they can be separate entities but make a striking combination when fused together.

Winston "Terry" Sutherland, PhD

Parenting constitutes being responsible for the children to whom we gave birth, adopt, or care for as our own. As legal guardians, we take care of our children by providing their basic needs—food, clothing, and shelter, let's say. When we work hard to provide food and prepare tasty meals for our children, we are participating in a basic parenting function. Similarly, when our daughter's high school teacher telephones to discuss her academic progress or classroom behavior, that discussion is a parenting activity.

Mentoring, on the other hand, tends to focus on the teaching, coaching, and guiding of the young. So while they are similar and may even be interrelated, mentoring has to do with our natural tendency to pass on our wealth of knowledge gained from having traveled this road before. When mom and dad prepare a meal for the kids, they are engaging in an act of parenting; but when they take it a step further by teaching them table etiquette, they may be engaging in an act of mentoring. They are mentoring them in the socially acceptable norms of the culture and thus setting them up for success in society. One area the need for mentoring may be obvious may be in matters that are not formally taught in the classroom. Such as those unspoken, loosely defined rules of suitable behavior in society. One example might be the bureaucracy one faces in public offices. Another is how to build meaningful relationships with the opposite sex. These are more akin to mentoring than they are to basic parenting; although, good parents are naturally good mentors.

Many of us were raised by well-meaning parents who worked hard to ensure we had a roof over our heads, clothes on our backs and food in our stomachs. Some of our parents provided little else in terms of teaching us the principles of successful living. And we may be raising our kids the same way; because, we tend to raise our children the way we were raised. But the problem with parenting only at the most basic level—providing food, clothing, and shelter—is that it only addresses the physical needs. As human beings, we are much more complex than mere physical beings. We are an intricately woven tapestry of social, spiritual, creative, and psychological wonders. When, as fathers, we fail to help Junior and Princess understand themselves in this equally complex world, they are left to grope around like a blind man in the dark.

> Defining mentoring is sort of tough, but describing it is pretty easy. It's like having an uncle that cares for you for a lifetime, and wants to see you do well. He's not your competitor; he's there to support you, not to compete with you or discourage you. He's not your critic as much as he is your cheerleader (Hendricks & Hendricks, 1995, p. 165).

Ideally, all fathers would be mentoring parents; but unfortunately, not all dads mentor their young. Many fall short of this important aspect of effective parenting. Mentoring shortens the time and minimizes the pains of trial-and-error learning so often experienced by the uninitiated. In other words, when fathers don't mentor their young, their children are left to figure out much of life for themselves, and this process of figuring out life for one's self involves trying different things until a good fit is found. This process may prove to be a costly obstacle course which, more often than not, leads to frustration for many. Even when fathers fail to make deliberate efforts to positively mentor their kids, they still influence their children's state of mind, their sense of confidence, and self-image. Fathers can't avoid teaching even if they tried; they still do it unawares. Fatherly influence occurs one way or the other, either for good or for bad. We cannot, not teach. Little children are giant sponges— soaking up everything going on around them. They observe everything we say and do, and take their cues from us, their elders. So whether we are aware of it or not, disengagement from the mentoring process has not hindered the transfer of information to them. Habits, attitudes, values, worldviews, and a host of other traits are still passed on; but unfortunately the impression they get, lead them to conclude that they must fend for themselves even while copying what they see in us. They subconsciously get it into their minds that they don't have a trustworthy guide in whom to confide. They feel they must go it alone. Psychologist Eric Berne packaged it well when he said, "Parents, deliberately or unaware, teach their children from birth how to behave, think, feel, and perceive. Liberation from these influences is no easy matter." Obviously, he is referring to a bad self-image which may be developed here; and such an image takes a long time to repair, if repair can be made at all. Unlearning bad habits is often more difficult than learning something new. It is much better to intentionally mentor our young and set the stage for them to enjoy a full and enriched life. As Frederick Douglas said, "It is easier to build strong children than to repair broken men."

Mentoring may be thought of as taming the mind, emotions, and passions. It is a training of the mind to organize, focus, and be efficient. It is a disciplining of the mind to control one's emotions and drives as opposed to being controlled by them. As wild horses need to be tamed in order to harness their enormous power, so people need to be taught manners and acceptable behavior and not be allowed to do whatever they feel to do at a given moment. Emotions, passions, impulses, and drives are not inherently bad; they're inherently powerful. Anything strong and powerful need to be managed lest they overpower us. The following narrative showcases one example of the power of fatherly mentoring.

A Mentoring Parent

Charles sat at the edge of his bed to tie his shoelaces—one of the many little habits he adopted from his father. 'Dad would be proud of my nomination for partnership at Sachs,' he thought to himself as a comforting smile snuck-up on his face then quickly disappeared. *Goldman Sachs* became the premier financial firm of his time. 'Uh, gumh!' Clearing his throat, his opposing thought replied, 'I have to be strong for the rest of the family,' as the lump in his throat betrayed his struggling attempts to keep a lid on his emotions. He was glad for the interruption when his wife of twenty-one years and three lovely children stuck her head through the bedroom door to remind him that uncle Othello would be arriving at any moment to drive them to the funeral service. Adjusting his tie in the mirror, he imagined his father staring back at him. Everyone always said how much he resembled his dad; this time there was no escaping the evidence, he couldn't deny his father's expressions etched on the contours of his own face.

The two shared a bond that would never be rivaled no matter which close friendships Charlie may develop. How is he to get through the eulogy this evening he wondered? He had lost more than a father; his dad became a confidant, adviser, supporter, mentor, cheerleader, and friend.

One of his earliest recollections occurred around six years old. It was one of those days when everything seemed to go wrong, even the weather felt damp and icky and Raggy the dog was snapping at anyone trying to play with him. Charlie remembered struggling to eat his vegetables that day. He shoveled a scoop of green peas into his mouth and began chewing, but all attempts at swallowing nauseated him resulting in him instinctively spitting them out. The green goo splattered against his dad's white, new shirt recently given to him as a birthday present from their mother. He had been saving it for a special occasion. Although not fully understanding, young Charles could sense that there was an air of specialness in his dad's preparations. Maybe it was the way he was humming his favorite song, *Good Morning Mr. Walker*, or the bounce in his step that gave Charles that sense. Of course, Charlie felt extremely distraught about soiling his father's new shirt and feared two things—a possible scolding and disappointing his father. He dreaded disappointing his father who meant so much to him. His wide open eyes, saddened expression, and fallen jaw revealed his concern.

But what made this incident memorable, and what later became recognized as one of his dad's trademark traits was how he managed the whole ordeal. At first, the ambush of wet, warm, mulch, splattering unexpectedly against him, momentarily caused him to tense-up his body and turn away his face grimacing. But after he recovered from that initial shock, he looked into Charlie's eyes, and with tender concern accompanying his voice, assured him that all was well, that he knew he couldn't help it. In fact, his disappointment about his soiled shirt quickly shifted to concern for Charlie's own struggle to swallow his vegetables. Charlie later overheard him planning to find out if it was an allergic reaction and if there was some other way he could get his nutrients until he was able to eat vegetables on his own. It was the sense that dad cared more about them than himself that cemented their bond over the years. For he, his siblings, and their mother, were the recipients of their father's strong but gentle approach to leading all his life.

Charlie recalled, as a young adult when he needed advice about which girl to ask out, how his father guided him in a way he could never come up with on his own in a million years. There were two girls who caught his attention, one at church and one at the university. The young lady at church was very attractive and polite but he felt she was a bit nosey and had a talent for gossip. The other girl at school was also good looking, although not as attractive as the one at church, intelligent, but didn't seem to have the family values he personally cherished. She was an independent woman who had her career path all marked out with no desire for a husband and children. Although neither of them became his wife, his dialogues with his father, particularly how he approached thinking through these sensitive matters, taught him how to confidently make choices when facing important decisions. One of the things he loved most was feeling that he was free to talk to his dad about anything without being judged.

Now he is facing the prospect of delivering his father's eulogy—the single greatest influence in his life. Earlier that day, he applied the finishing touches to what he planned to read that evening. He would be careful to do a good job of honoring his father's legacy. The following is an excerpt of what he planned to say.

Alan Edward Cummings was born on March 10th, 1959 to Errol and Marcy Cummings in the Caribbean island of Trinidad. Alan attended *St. Agnes Anglican School* and *Queens Royal College* before immigrating to the United States in 1973. Upon his arrival to New York, Alan did a number of odd jobs before accepting a position at a hospital where he stayed for the rest of his life. In his last position there, he served as a head lab technician; and although he had both the ambition and several offers to enter medical school, he declined in order to work overtime and concentrate on providing educational opportunities for his kids. Dad made sure that we had a stable home. He was the consummate family man. That he loved mom and each of his children more than he loved himself was obvious for all to see. He got his greatest joy from seeing his family healthy, and happy. Dad believed in living a balanced life. "Balance" was one of his favorite words he used over and over again. He maintained a set of guiding principles by which he lived his life and passed on to each of us. It was not enough for him to be a good provider and protector; dad wanted us to be happy, confident, respectful, and respected. He was concerned about our overall wellbeing both individually and collectively. If I could be half the man he was, I would have lived a complete life. He taught us how to be good human beings. My wife always tells people I won her heart because I knew how to treat a lady. Dad made sure we were gentlemen. He said the world could never have too many gentlemen. He taught me how to shave, how to tie a tie, how to dance with a lady, and how to wait for the right moment to speak and act.

Alan Edward Cummings, "Lovey" as he was affectionately called, left to cherish his memory, his loving wife Kathleen, three children Charles, Colin, and Ann; his brother James, his sister Carol, and a host of cousins and grandchildren.

This anecdote highlights the mentoring aspects of coaching and guidance provided by Lovey based on the affection he held for Charles and his siblings. He viewed his parenting role as that of both father and mentor. Not only did he provide their basic needs of food, clothing, and shelter, he also supplied a hefty dose of life-coaching.

This next narrative lacked the life-coaching throughout the individual's upbringing. All basic needs were provided by her parents but her father was not particularly a mentoring parent.

A Non-Mentoring Parent

Nicole is the sweetest young lady you will ever meet. It doesn't matter what type of day she is having, you can count on her to greet you with a sunshine smile and the heartiest of hellos. She'd sacrifice anything to ensure you have what you need. It bothers her to disappoint anyone so she goes out of her way to avoid letting people down. Her own happiness, however, may too often be called into question. She complains about meeting the wrong kind of men who regularly lie to her and take her for granted. But she seems unable to break her habit of returning to the sort of guys who scrounge money off her, who disappear for weeks and return with very detailed and convincing stories that have little to do with the truth and who physically and verbally abuse her. She is tired of meeting Mr. Wrong but she doesn't feel that the kind of quality guy she wants will want her too. That is how she truly feels about herself. Her sense of self-worth isn't very high. That she didn't complete high school hasn't helped matters either. How she feels about herself, rightly or wrongly, colors the decisions she makes in choosing a mate and everything she does. Even her tendency to be kind to others may in part, result from her belief that it is the only way she will get people to like her because she feels she has nothing else to offer. Her perception of herself—that she doesn't have much to bring to the bargaining table—has clearly affected her decision-making skills when it comes to the guys she dates and the jobs she takes.

Both of Nicole's parents were physically present in the home but they took little interest in her overall development as a person. Of course, she never lacked for food, clothing, and shelter; but she was left to interpret life for herself. When she entered teenage years, she was glued to the television and was fascinated with pop culture's glitter; she drank-in a daily dose of MTV, Entertainment Tonight, and VH1. She never felt safe to share her innermost thoughts with her parents. In fact, they made light of her interests in fashion, boys, and her career choice. Nicole struggled to complete her schoolwork having had no help from her parents who instead suggested she was not college material. So although she was their sweet little girl, their lack of mentoring failed to provide her the very best start she could have in this tricky world.

The people in our care need to be assured that there is nothing they can do to diminish our love and loyalty to them. Having said that, however, a gentle caveat may be warranted. This does not mean that they are now granted license to abuse our good graces; it is meant to affirm their value and reinforce the sense of security and love bestowed upon them. We will always find people who will violate our trust and mishandle our kindnesses. But when it comes to our young, it should not prevent us from leaving no doubt in their minds that they are loved. Charles Swindoll published a book called, *The Grace Awakening*—a play on words from that era in American history known as the "The Great Awakening." In his chapter appropriately titled "Isn't Grace Risky?" he discussed the tendency we have of abusing the latitude provided us when grace is offered. Grace is risky to the persons extending the courtesy; they open themselves to misuse. But this is a risk worth taking. The young people we mentor are much more valuable than the misplaced abuse our graces will endure. They need our mature, balanced, and loving guidance.

Parenting and mentoring although similar may be distinguished by the additional step of providing guidance to our young, coaching them through the game of life so they are poised for a fair chance at life success. One of the greatest battlefields both Junior and Princess will face concerns their sense of self—their identity. They will have to contend with and confront themselves. That ongoing conversation they will have with themselves about themselves; whether they like themselves, how they deal with praise and criticism can either make or break them. The landscapes of their inner selves are necessary frontiers for dad to explore when thinking of how to best guide his young.

Winston "Terry" Sutherland, PhD

Chapter 3

Dad's Influence of Affirmation: *Being Approved in Identity*

Be what you is, not what you ain't, 'cause if you ain't what you is,
you is what you ain't.

—Luther Price

Conversations With Myself

As we move through life's stages, we engage in identity checks along the way. And even though two stages in particular, puberty and middle age, are better-known than their counterparts, we actually experience mini identity-crises at more turns than we're willing to admit. When, for instance, twelve year old Junior is reduced to tears because no kid on the playground picked him to play on their team, might he not be dealing with identity issues? He may be brought face to face with his own sense of value to the group. "Am I good enough for them? Or maybe I'm only good enough for the other group which didn't quite make it playing over on the other side?" If, at twenty eight, he struggles to hold down a job or maintain relationships, these have the potential to adversely affect his sense of self.

At each stage we may engage in conscious and subconscious self-talk about who we are. For many, this private conversation can go on forever. And some never quite accept themselves for who they are as they struggle with their self-worth and reputations. Others may have less of a struggle because they both know and like themselves; therefore, they face life with confidence and enjoy more of the gift of life we've been granted.

In this chapter we explore dad's influence of affirmation where mentored children are being approved in their identities. This reassuring influence renders kids "at peace" with themselves. To set the stage for this discussion, please allow the utility of a modern-day fairytale.

To Be Or Not To Be?

The blockbuster movie *Shrek II* erupted onto our screens with the newlywed ogres, Shrek and Fiona, enraptured in honeymoon bliss. But before the ink on the marriage certificate had time to dry, Fiona's parents sent a delegation of messengers inviting them to a royal ball. When they arrived, they were greeted by Fiona's parents and right away the tensions were evident. Both parents were clearly disappointed with the identity of Fiona's husband. They had been banking on Prince Charming as a son-in-law for their daughter. But alas, it was an ogre which lived in a swamp.

At some point, Shrek learned that the Fairy Godmother's "Happily-Ever-After" potion can change his appearance into something adorable. And since his physical appearance seemed to be the cause of all his unhappiness, he was counting on this potion to solve his problems. He conspires to get it.

But now that he held it in his hands with all its promise of bliss, he thought long and hard about what he was about to do. The seriousness of a changed identity began to hit home to him. He thought about what he would be giving up to become somebody else. For, although he was a lowly ogre, he was quite happy with himself. He liked who he was; he wasn't interested in being anyone else but himself, unflattering in his appearance or not. His predicament? He could either risk losing Fiona, the love of his life, or he could risk losing an important part of his identity. "To be? Or, not to be?" That was the question! After grappling with this dilemma for a while, Shrek decided to go through with it; he took the potion and fell asleep under its spell. When he awoke, he found himself gloriously transformed into a handsome gentleman basking in the adulation of beautiful women. The bottle now empty, Shrek noticed additional instructions written on the backside of the label stating that, to make the changes permanent, he must kiss the love of his life by midnight.

Believing that this was what Fiona wanted, he made the ultimate sacrifice. He hunted her down and when he found her, leaned forward to kiss her just before midnight. But Fiona stopped him and explained that she does want to live happily-ever-after but, "... with the ogre I married."

Relieved and overjoyed, Shrek can now truly live happily ever after. He can be who he was meant to be without the pressure of being somebody else. He doesn't have to worry about something going wrong in the future and embarrassingly reverting back to being an ogre. He was free to be himself.

Although this story was steeped in fantasy and fairytale, like any good work of fiction, the *Shrek* tale mirrors reality. And while many merely took away the entertainment value of the movie, the undercurrents of personal identity was refreshing to film enthusiasts. Great works of fiction can provoke sober thought about deep life issues. And the producers of *Shrek* provided audiences opportunity to reflect upon the value of their identity.

Junior and Princess will be wrestling with the central question of this story, "to be or not to be?" i.e. to stay true to themselves or to pull off the biggest fraud of their lives by pretending to be someone else. They will encounter many opportunities to follow the crowd and be someone they're not, in order to gain acceptance and approval. This peer-pressure is not confined to the better known teenage years; the pressure to conform to the group's dictates and to become what family, friends, and society demand continues throughout a person's lifetime. Dad may help stabilize their identities by helping them accept who they are and feel great about themselves.

Seeking Affirmation

Deep within, kids subconsciously seek affirmation of who they are. That simple but highly influential gesture from dad to validate his children's sense of identity satisfies their need for approval. As Junior grows and explores both himself and his surroundings, he constantly tries to make sense of who he is and how he fits into the jigsaw puzzle of life. And when his parents say something that confirms the way he feels about himself—especially if it is positive—he then feels validated and affirmed. Naturally the validation of negative thoughts and feelings may be reinforced by dad as well. These can leave deep and lasting scars upon the young. So it is especially important to validate their positive thinking. This validation is important because it provides grounding in kids' minds. Like an anchor, affirmation provides stability. It boosts kids' fickle confidence. In spite of the indifference many teenagers show, they care deeply about what their parents think of them, say to them, and do with them.

We've all had the experience of seeing children excitedly demand their parents' attention. "Look daddy, I'm strong; feel my muscles!" "See how pretty I look in this dress, daddy?" "Come outside, daddy; watch me climb this tree!" But is this merely seeking attention? Aren't they really craving affirmation about who they are? They want to hear the magic words. They want to hear how good they are. Better yet, they want to hear that dad is pleased with them. They want to be validated in how they view themselves and how we view them. They are very aware of their lack of size and lack of strength and can easily feel like they don't matter very much. They can't wait to grow up to be "big" (that's their word, BIG!) so they can equally be recognized and matter. Obviously, they're not only physically small but more importantly they also feel marginalized and insignificant.

I can't think of anything crueler than being ignored, taken for granted, and treated as unconscious when you're as conscious as the next guy. And that's what they're fighting for, recognition, validation, and affirmation. Medical doctors told of a time they were treating a man who had been comatose for three years. The patient was declared unconscious. During one of her rounds monitoring his condition, the doctor recognized that for several months the patient had been moving his eyes. It was later determined that he was trying to indicate that he was conscious. He could hear their medical chatter but there was no way he could get them to notice that he was conscious. One day the breakthrough happened. When they attached several magnetic transmitters to his head and sourced them to a computer he was able to send them certain signals which alerted them to his conscious state. Could you think of anything worse than being conscious and treated like you're unconscious? Ignored kids feel invisible and like this patient—conscious, but treated as though they're unconscious; there, but as if they're not there. Every opportunity they get to prove that they matter will be exploited; so they seek out their parents' affirmation. Attentive fathers pick up on this and are careful not to deprive their children of this important affirmation.

In the *Survey of Fatherly Influence*, sixty-three percent of the respondents said that the words they would most like to hear their fathers say to them are "I'm proud of you." These are words of affirmation and they go a long way in approving and validating a kid's sense of identity. To be proud of your children and tell them so meets one of the great identity grounding needs in a child's life.

Without a good understanding of our children's unique individuality, getting them to relate to family, community, and the world will be like spitting against the wind. That's how important it is to take the time to understand your child. We can't get the best out of Junior and Princess if we don't understand them. Nor can we get them to flourish into the best they can be. No one runs their best in another person's shoes. What could be worse than being forced to live out the expectations of parents when a child's makeup is totally opposite to those expectations? Each person born on this planet is one-of-a-kind, special, distinct, and peculiar. This ought to be celebrated. How fascinating to know that there never was, neither is there now, nor will there ever be another identical to me. And there is no other individual anywhere who has ever lived who is quite like your child. It is therefore very important to take time to study her as much as she will spend the rest of her life trying to understand herself. Fathers do their kids a disservice when they call them "weird" and snicker at the seemingly strange things they think, wear, listen to, like, and do. They're different, young, and imaginative. Their creative and imaginative minds are full of wonder and it doesn't take much for them to be awestruck. Wise fathers encourage them both to dream and to pursue their dreams. Mentoring dads, aware of their enormous influence, never attempt to clone themselves in their children; instead, they promote and celebrate their kids' beautiful and unique personalities. I am convinced that MANY fathers trigger-off a massive "shut-down" of their children's creative channels. As one celebrated high school principal noted, "Parents kill more dreams than anybody." By throwing cold water on their attempts at new things which didn't come off quite right, kids' sensitive spirits may be crushed and they could develop a cynical outlook on life. This affects how they view themselves because dad's approval means more to them than they're aware of. They may not be aware that they're seeking identity validation; but the absence of dad's affirmation can create a bottomless pit of unanswered questions which can only be satisfied by a father's genuine validation.

What Is Identity?

So what are we talking about here? The dictionary says identity is, "The fact of being who or what a person or thing is." That's it. It's that simple and that complicated. Too many people aren't allowed to be themselves. And as a consequence, some spend a great part of their lives trying to "find themselves." When seeking to understand one's identity we're asking the question, who are you? It remains one of life's big questions. We are seeking to understand a person's sense of self. This is of great importance because people's perceptions of their own unique individuality form the basis for how they live out their lives. And kids' perceptions of themselves will have great effect on whether they enjoy life or struggle through it.

Of all the possible factors which make up a person's identity, two broad forces may account for shaping us into who we are—nature and nurture. Nature here refers to the personalized genetic code with which each of us was born, those unique physical attributes which are undeniably you. No one on earth has quite the same physical appearance you have. Your face, voice, height, color, bone structure, hair texture, the way you walk, are all particular to you. Nurture on the other hand, refers to our upbringing; the manner by which we were raised—the home culture, our parent's philosophy, the attitudes and the behaviors which may be adopted from home and community.

These two forces of genetics and environment conspire together to create the persons we eventually become. So when it comes to affecting behavior the question becomes, which has the greater influence? Do we tend to do the things we do because of our genetic code, or as a result of outside influences such as traditions passed on to us and the culture we're a part of? Many believe we are who we are as a result of the combination of both nature and nurture. So, although there are personality types such as extraverts and introverts, our upbringing also contributes to our overall personality and by extension our identity.

Once again the greatest influence remains the home. Therefore, when attempting to understand Junior and Princess' identities, it is helpful to take into account the whole person: his unique physical appearance, her personal tastes, their home life, and general culture to name a few. One's identity constitutes the essence of who she is in totality and each one is as distinct as each snowflake is unique.

It is this uniqueness which may either pose a problem or be a blessing to Princess and Junior. On the one hand they will eventually assert their independence and showcase their special differences but they first need to feel part of the group. They will gain confidence to display their unique differences when they embrace and accept themselves for who they are. The more they are affirmed and approved in their identities; the more confident and expressive they will be about themselves.

Identity And Self-Esteem

During one of my courses, we discussed the importance of identity and self-perception. Before the discussion got underway, the professor had us answer the question, who am I? We were instructed to complete the statement, "I am_____" in as many ways as we can.

Before we proceed, I invite you to place a marker at this point in your reading; take a moment to close the book and engage in this exercise. You can either do it mentally or you can write them down. It is probably best to write them down. Then we will continue our discussion on this topic. Go ahead, close the book and complete that statement in as many ways as you can. "I am _____."

Good! How was the experience?

Many of the guys wrote down things like, I am a man, I am handsome, I am a computer technician, I am a father, I am a history buff, etcetera. The women wrote things like, I am a woman, I am a wife, I am a mother of two lovely kids, I am exhausted, and so on. The men tended to identify themselves with their occupations; the women thought of themselves in relation to their children and spouses. Neither of the answers is wrong or right, good or bad; they merely reveal something about how we perceive ourselves. The exercise also revealed that most people are poor students of themselves—they compiled very short lists.

Finding the answer to that question, however, is not necessarily a simple feat. Who we are involves a complex network interwoven together to make a complete individual. And sons and daughters all over the planet are attempting to answer this elusive question, who am I? They, like us, will spend the rest of their lives revising their positions on who they are. Whether they are aware of it or not, they're looking to their parents for clues. Fathers can help guide them to a "self" they will love and one in whom they will be proud.

Anecdotes illustrating the crucial influence a strong sense of identity has upon an individual may prove helpful.

One of the frequent questions Jesus faced when He walked our planet was, "who are you?" Everybody, the Pharisees, Sadducees, Roman governors, and the regular folks were more than a little curious to know His true identity. Interestingly, the answer to that question made all the difference in how He was received. But more importantly for us, our interest isn't so much about how Jesus was treated; rather, a more telling observation reveals how He lived His life as a result of knowing who He was. And this may be the greatest value in understanding and embracing one's identity—it can have great positive effect on how we live our lives.

John's Gospel records an event which grants rare insight into the immense value of knowing your identity and the power, freedom, and contentment this knowledge provides. It is the well known incident of Jesus washing His disciples' feet.

The dusty streets of that region were well travelled on foot and on caravans of donkeys, horses, and camels prevalent during that time. But the average sojourner didn't have access to these, they walked. It was therefore customary to have ready, a jar of water at their homes' entrance for the purpose of washing their guests' feet as a courtesy. Now, nobody is thrilled to handle the mucky, grimy, callused feet of grown men. No one volunteers for this job. A servant was usually provided to do this dirty chore; on this occasion, none was provided. The mood in that room must have been a combination of tiredness because of the long, physically taxing journey and excitement as it was the occasion of the most revered festival in the Jewish calendar—the Passover feast. One could easily picture Peter, James, and John thinking, "I'm not washing anybody's feet; I didn't sign up for that." Then the unexpected happened. Jesus decided to do the scorned deed and wash the feet of His disciples as one of the last things He did before returning to His father. (By the way, have you ever had someone of very high regard serve you? I often wonder what these men were thinking and how they felt when Jesus stooped to take their filthy feet in His hands. One by one He methodically attended to each of them including Judas who, that very night, literally sold Him out to His enemies.) With towel in hand, He poured water into a bowl and attended to His mentees' mucky feet.

This may not readily appear to be such a big deal to many, but upon closer scrutiny it speaks volumes about Jesus and the role His self-knowledge played in His life. Remember, Jesus was not their equal; He was their leader, their Lord. This shocking act may be comparable to the Queen of England cleaning her servants' toilets or something of that sort. Wouldn't that be an awkward sight? If anything, the role is reversed; servants clean for their masters, disciples serve their Lord. But of course, the chasm between Jesus and His disciples is infinitely wider than the gap between royalty and servants. It is John who helps us to grasp the significance of Jesus' actions.

In the opening lines of his Gospel, John reported that Jesus was actually the creator of all things who later became human and lived among His own creatures. It is this sobering thought to which John fastened his argument when he said in chapter 13, verse 3, immediately before the feet washing incident: *Jesus knew that the father had put all things under His power, and that He had come from God and was returning to God.* Before John described the events of that fateful night, he felt it necessary to tell his readers what Jesus *knew about Himself.* In other words, John wanted his readers to understand that Jesus was secure in His identity; He knew who He was. He knew His history, and His future. He knew where He came from and where He was going. He knew His pedigree. He knew His identity.

So Jesus was willing to do servants' work because He knew that such tasks didn't define who He was; they didn't mean He was a mere servant; He was still their Lord and Creator of all things. His position, both in God's eyes and those of his disciples, was not compromised. No one left there thinking any less of Jesus. His value was not diminished because of stooping to wash the dirty feet of imperfect men who were about to betray Him and deny that they even knew Him. His "Stock" did not fall. In fact, in the eyes of His followers, His value increased; they revered Him more.

The better people understand who they are, the more confident they tend to be when sizing up lofty goals. And they tend to be equally "at-peace" with doing the menial tasks others fear will demean them. When we are secure in our identities, we don't mind doing the things society, friends, and associates find degrading. Shame, embarrassment, and low self-esteem often accompany the insecure individual. Though many, insecure in their identities, fear they may draw the scorns and snarls of onlookers; others, comfortable with who they are, know that these things don't define them. We are who we are and will remain who we are in spite of the tasks we must sometimes perform. Does it make me less of a person if I take out the garbage, and vacuum the floors of hotels? Or does it make me more of a person if I run a sophisticated operation and make lots of money? The answer to this of course, is a resounding no!

This reminds me of a British missionary who served in a developing country. Locals had been wary of the droves of haughty, pompous, and pretentious missionaries who set themselves above the nationals. But this missionary was different. Nigel didn't elevate himself above the people he came so many miles to serve; instead, he was found visiting and socializing with many of the locals. One native, with eyes aglow and jaw dropped in shock, told of the time she came to like and respect Nigel. She explained that their church was hosting a conference and volunteers from the group were helping to prepare the building for the event. While washing the windows, she noticed Nigel cleaning the bathrooms with hands fully submerged in the bowl giving it a good clean. What stuck with me from this story was the impact it had on, not only this national, but many others as well. Everyone who knew him commented on his humility, likeableness, authenticity, and trustworthiness. Volunteering to perform menial tasks didn't make Nigel appear less valuable or less respected by the people he came to serve—they made him more respected. He couldn't do this if he was insecure in his identity.

Embracing your identity liberates you to be yourself. When people are "at-home" in their own skins, they tend to have less stress and live happier, more fulfilling lives. They don't permit negative thoughts like shame, guilt, and discouragement to dampen their spirits. Those thoughts, more often than not, carry with them messages not coded with the truth. They are designed to discourage and derail us from realizing our full potential. Being comfortable with our identities allows us to be at peace with who we are. It anchors us to a solid foundation from which informed choices may be made. It engenders pride, good pride, not arrogance. It prevents us from envying others because we're content with who we are and the things we have. It leaves no breeding ground for inferiority complexes. When the arrogant speak in condescending tones to us, we do not whimper under their toothless intimidation tactics; we rather transcend the folly of their feeble attempts at breaking us down.

This underscores the value of affirming Junior and Princess in their identities. They need to know and be proud of their heritage. Thy neither need to be ashamed of their background nor insecure about themselves. They ought to be right at home in their own skins, both when alone and around others. Great dads validate their children's sense of identity. They're careful not to crush their spirits. They resist any temptations to minimize their individuality. They break negative habits that may have been handed down to them from their childhood home. If their parents criticized and chided them with put-downs, they try to avoid repeating the same. They perfume their tones, words, and facial expressions with non-judgmental and encouraging tones, words, and expressions. They uphold a positive outlook on their kids' physical appearance and their yet imperfect contributions when they try. These fathers understand that their kids' self-esteem is directly linked to how they will think and feel about themselves. Dads have a wonderful opportunity to make it a bright, sunshiny, self-image. When children are secure in their identities they will more likely flourish in life and be better poised to fulfill their potential. Dorothy Law Nolte, the late family counselor and author of the poem, *Children Learn What They Live*, may have said it best when she penned the timeless words:

If children live with criticism, they learn to condemn
If children live with shame, they learn to feel guilty
If children live with encouragement, they learn confidence
If children live with approval, they learn to like themselves

Promoting and uplifting Junior and Princess' self-esteem will create a never-ending power source they can access throughout their lifetimes.

Since our sense of identity is central to who we are, and a great part is connected to outside social factors; as social beings we tend to be concerned with how others think and feel about us—our reputations.

Identity And Reputation

It has been said that "We are not what we think we are. We are not even what others think we are. We are what we think others think we are." This curious observation highlights the undeniable preoccupation we have with others' opinions of us. While some people don't obsess about what others think about them, there may be a healthy amount of consideration given to how we are perceived by others. And many of us find ourselves attempting to live up to what we think others expect of us.

A well-known proverb says, "A good name is better to have than great riches." In a capitalistic/materialistic society like ours, many may consider that statement laughable. To be clear, however, this saying is not referring to our actual name given to us by our parents at birth; instead, it refers to one's reputation. The idea is that having a good reputation is more important than pocketing lots of money—especially if it means one must endure scorn and be the laughingstock of his community. Such a person has a bad name, a bad reputation. Some may even be blacklisted. And few things are more difficult to repair than a soiled reputation. A quick glance at fallen celebrities the likes of golfer Tiger Woods, former U.S. President Bill Clinton, singer Whitney Houston, Cyclist Lance Armstrong, and actress Lindsay Lohan speaks volumes about the cost of a tainted reputation. If I were a betting man I'd be willing to make a wager on the notion that Tiger Woods, for instance, would give almost anything to erase the public's opinion of him with regard to the broadcasted adulterous events which led to his divorce. Former President Bill Clinton will forever have the Monica Lewinsky incident which led to his impeachment as that dark blot on his otherwise stellar record. Beloved singer and rhythm & blues diva, the late Whitney Houston, may have paid the ultimate price for her foray into a life of illicit drugs. Lance Armstrong deceived the public by acquiring the prestigious Tour de France cycling medals while using banned substances. Consequently, he has been stripped of all his titles and he must now pay back millions of endorsement dollars. Benjamin Franklin may have said it best, "Glass, china, and reputation are easily crack'd and never well mended." Even if all the kings' horses and all the kings' men tried, they couldn't put Humpty Dumpty back together again. Our reputations, like our names are tied to our identities.

This is clearly observed in the relationship between banks and their customers. When Junior meets "miss wonderful" and decides it's time to purchase a home, banks will want to know the state of his financial reputation. They will access his record of borrowing and repaying to see the history of his financing habits. This information is readily available through credit bureaus. And good credit is what banks rely on when deciding to grant loans to borrowers; the credit report serves as a record of the reputation we have with banks.

Unfortunately, identity theft has become epidemic over the last few years with access to our most personal information made easy with the click of a mouse. Countless victims have lost their homes. Unsuspecting marriages have ended in divorce. And mayhem has visited many because of stolen identities. Many people therefore, spend years attempting to rebuild their financial reputations after an imposter gets hold of their identities and misrepresents them all over town. Victims, having discovered that someone had been impersonating them, are devastated. I once heard a victim describe the unpleasant experience as a feeling of invasion into her most private places—like an uninvited guest rummaging through the drawer where her underwear is kept.

Our reputations may also come under scrutiny when applying for a job. Human resource professionals routinely investigate several sources to ensure that the person they're considering hiring is reputable. Apart from checking the wonderful references we provide them, they also launch inquiries into previous places of employment, social networking sites like Facebook, and databases containing information on law infringement and sex offenders, among other sources.

Besides those formal establishments shining a searchlight on Junior and Princess' reputations, informal but equally important institutions monitor their reputations as well. Church relationships, relationships with immediate and extended family, coworkers, and friends if not properly managed can greatly tarnish their names. If for instance, they have a habit of not keeping their word, borrowing and never returning what they borrowed, always arriving late to work or functions, these will invariably affect the level of respect they receive, and whether they will be taken seriously.

What makes a ruined reputation so bad is that it strikes at the core of a person's honor. To be disgraced and dishonored is a sort of death to a cherished part of our lives. When people lose everything, one of the few vestiges of value they cling to is their dignity. When you've lost that, you may feel like you've finally lost everything; the feeling of hopelessness and haunting shame may cripple you, hammering the last nail into your coffin, making it hard to lift up your head in public. Right along with faith and hope are dignity and honor and these go a long way in defining us. Therefore, our names become one and the same with our reputations which in turn are closely tied to our identities.

Affirming Junior's Identity

Mentoring fathers know their value to their children's identity. Equally important, they know the value of their children's sense of identity. Dads' understanding and embracing their role in their kids' lives is perhaps the first step in any good mentoring approach. This privilege is granted, neither to the teacher, the government, the religious leader, the best friend, nor the sports hero but to the parent. NBA hall-of-famer Charles Barkley was right, he is not our children's ideal role model—we are. Dad's task is to make sure that when Junior and Princess think about themselves, good thoughts flood their minds. A person's self-image is like a trusted, loyal, and beloved friend who is always there. Few things could be more critical to their happiness.

I once heard of a father and daughter who enjoyed a particularly good relationship. But the daughter was born with a birthmark covering the left side of her face. When she was still quite young, the time came for her to attend school. The other kids saw her and started to call her all sorts of demeaning names as kids everywhere do. (Kids can say some of the meanest things.) She simply wanted to make friends like everybody else. Feeling dejected by the ridicule she received at the hands of her classmates, she ran into her father's arms and told him how horrible her first day went and how the other children taunted her. The father wisely comforted his precious little girl, building up her sense of value and confidence so much so that when he was done with her the daughter felt sorry for the other kids because they didn't have a special mark like hers. He affirmed her sense of worth and validated her identity. Dad took that nightmare and turned it into a dream. Princess isn't supposed to walk away from such a potentially traumatic incident feeling that somehow she isn't quite as valued as anyone else. Fathers can create an atmosphere of optimism in their kids' hearts. This dad understood his role in affirming his child's sense of identity.

A bit of caution may be warranted here. Power of any kind must be handled thoughtfully; we're not to abuse our influence over them. The well known adage, "Power corrupts; absolutely power corrupts absolutely," may not be taken lightly. The influence father wields in his kids' trusting hearts lodges deep and is embedded permanently in their psyche. They should be responsible with their influence over how their children think and feel about themselves. They should be careful not to force their own "way" upon any of their children. If tempted, dads should resist the urge to vicariously live their lives through their kids. Dads had their time and their own lives; this is Junior and Princess' time, it's their lives. Any molding, shaping, or influencing ought to be carefully approached taking Junior and Princess' unique tendencies and bents into consideration.

The popular adage, "Train up a child in the way he should go, and when he is old he will not depart from it," may have been misunderstood by many. Parents traditionally understood the phrase "the way he should go" to mean the straight-and-narrow way. And while the collective voice of scripture prescribes that everyone takes the straight and narrow way, these words in this context may be concerned with a different issue. Could it be that the emphasis here is upon parents paying attention to Junior and Princess' natural bents and basic interests? In other words, parents should not impose "someone else's way" upon them but train them up in the way "they" should go—their own God-given way. In this context, their "way" does not refer to their fallen nature or depravity; but to their own unique style of doing things. It does not refer to their rebellious knack for getting into trouble, but to their special way that makes them different. So when training them up, be sure to do so in the way "they" should go. Train them up in the way of things in which they've shown a consistent pattern of behavior, tendencies, aptitude, and interest. When this is done, they will not depart from it.

Well-meaning dads may have dropped the ball at this crucial juncture. Because of their zeal in attempting to fulfill their paternal calling, many emphasize the straight and narrow while stifling Junior and Princess' spirit and sense of identity in the process. One simple way to test this is to track the outcome of the prediction. In other words, when fathers worked hard and made sure they trained up Junior and Princess in the straight-and-narrow way is it true that they never depart from that way when they are old? That's the test. If the truth be told, countless fathers are frustrated because despite their best efforts, many of their children abandon both their faith and their father's ways. But when they pay attention to their kids' unique temperament, "their way" and continue to steer them along that way in which they should go, they never depart from it. This is so because they're their God-given way. This may be akin to another old adage which says, "don't try to force a square peg into a round hole!"

There is an exercise which illustrates one aspect of a person's natural tendencies. It does not reveal all of her ways but it serves to demonstrate that we do indeed have a natural preference for doing things. In this exercise, participants are asked to take a pen or pencil and write their names using the hand with which they don't usually write. Then they are asked to repeat the exercise switching to the hand with which they regularly write. I encourage you to participate in this exercise. Go ahead; take a moment to do this. If you haven't tried this before, it may surprise you. After participants have written their names with both hands, they are asked to reveal both the product of what they wrote and to discuss the experience. Not surprisingly, most people are right-handed, that is, they do most things with their right hand. So when they described writing their names with their left hand they described the experience as very uncomfortable, taking longer, and the letters looking like they've been blindfolded and stricken with chronic arthritis. But when they switched to their right hands, their natural way, they wrote comfortably, faster, and the letters looked normal. Much like this simple demonstration, we all have certain preferred ways of thinking, feeling, and behaving that are natural to us. Forcing any other way upon Junior may bring confusion to his sense of identity. It is much better to seek to understand him and build upon the foundation of his natural, God-given bents.

One of the things mentoring fathers are keenly aware of involves knowing how their children think and feel about themselves. How children perceive themselves, whether accurately or inaccurately, will affect everything they do. Perception is reality in the eyes of the perceiver. As Anais Nin observed, "We don't see things as they are; we see them as we are." Our state of being—our happiness, sadness, contentment, discontentment, our general frame of mind, whether we esteem ourselves or struggle with low self-image, are all tied to our identity.

How we think of ourselves will be manifested in our choices and behaviors. The careers we pursue are influenced by our self-perception. The places we frequent reflect the associations with which we're comfortable. The friends with whom we mingle are a reflection of our social identity. It has been said, "Show me your friends and I will tell you who you are." The saying, "clothes make a man" betrays the impression we make by our choice of attire. The cars we drive have often been used as either a barometer of our financial worth, a status-symbol, or as an extension of our egos. The list is as inexhaustible as the clichés are endless. When it comes to food, it is said—you are what you eat. The music we listen to and the places we live are all subject to how we think, feel, and view ourselves. These are all outward manifestations of an inward reality—an ongoing, personal conversation with ourselves.

Our young need to know their history so they may have the proper background to understand themselves and fashion a fine future. They have a sense of where they came from, what they came through, and have confidence in where they are heading. They need to know and like who they are. There must be no question in their minds that they are loved, that they are valuable, that they are precious. These virtues are critical to shaping their sense of self-image which will enable them to stand firm when they must make the unpopular but right choices in life.

Tied to many daughters' identity is their father's place in their lives. He is usually the first man they will ever love. So when they're ready to choose a husband, their measuring stick is their father. Of course, the same phenomenon is true for boys and their mothers. When considering a life partner, he subconsciously looks for certain traits reminiscent of his mother. But they look to their father to interpret how to live with and love a woman. Proven and timeless principles may be passed on to our kids—like choosing one's friends wisely, and learning how to manage one's emotions.

It is a fascinating experience to observe a sculptor at work on his sculpture and marvel at the way he carefully takes his time when shaping the physical identity of his artwork. He either has a replica he is trying to reproduce on wood, stone, ice, clay, or some other solid material; or he has an image in his mind to which he's attempting to give physical expression—its own personal identity. With chisel in hand, he skillfully chips away anything that doesn't belong on the finished product. In the same way, mentoring fathers work to shape their children's psychological, social, and spiritual identity. They constantly chip away the unseemly parts that wrinkle their child's finished personality. From the earliest influences upon junior's overall personality all the way to young-adulthood, the appropriate carving and molding may be provided. Of course, there are some things beyond dad's reach. The lad's anatomy, biology, and temperament may be fixed.

But other external influences may be maneuvered to favor the child's best positioning for a healthy and happy life. Much of the shaping occurs during the child's formative years—from infancy to around sixteen years of age—their impressionable minds like sponges soak up much of the family culture. If dad is proactive and not passive, those forces of nurture can be manipulated to work for the good of his precious children.

Fathers occupy the most strategically advantageous position to establish Junior and Princess' healthy self-image. To pull this off, however, they create a safe environment within which their families may flourish. They are aware of their role in affirming and validating their children. The mentoring dad helps positively influence his child's sense of identity. Since the home has the strongest impact upon children and since kids' sense of identity determine their state of mind, father must maximize his influence upon his young by exercising loving leadership.

Winston "Terry" Sutherland, PhD

Chapter 4

Dad's Influence of Affection: *Being A Loving Leader*

I will pay more for the ability to deal with people than any other ability under the sun.
—John D. Rockefeller

Fatherly Leadership Not Optional

In Junior High, boys took a vocational course in either auto mechanics or woodworking. Girls enrolled in home economics which taught them cooking, and sewing. I ended up in Mr. Grant's woodworking class where we learned to make benches, tables, ashtrays and piggybanks among other things. One day Mr. Grant was called into the office to answer an important telephone call. (Now, except for the futuristic television series *Star Trek*, in those days the cellular phone wasn't yet in widespread use.) When he returned, he was shocked at what he saw. Prior to his leaving the classroom, it was orderly and peaceful; but when he returned, pieces of wood were flying through the air—he had to dodge two or three times to avoid being clobbered in the head. The noise level was deafening. Students were fighting with each other. Desks and chairs had been overturned on their sides. The entire workshop was in a state of chaos—all because the leader left the room of hot-blooded teenagers besieged by raging hormones. I always think back to that incident and marvel at how quickly conditions can go from relative peace and stability to full-blown upheaval. I never forgot what happens when leadership is either absent, passive, or broken down.

A state of anarchy describes the condition of a society which has lost its ability to govern. It is a breakdown in leadership characterized by a sharp rise in criminal activity. During those chaotic times, citizens display great disregard for the law. Chaos and disorder bulldoze any unprotected structures standing in their paths. This unwelcomed imposter of failed leadership has visited not only nations, states, and cities but also many homes around the world. As a result, the threat of anarchy looms large and provides a compelling reason for dads to provide proper leadership.

The dictionary defines a leader as one who: guides by going before or with; has influence; is or goes at the head of; is a route to a place; or, is in an advanced position of others. Based on these, leadership entails providing guidance by going ahead of or with them, influencing them, keeping several steps ahead of them, being a conduit or a route for them, and occupying an advanced position of them.

So it is not enough for a teacher to be knowledgeable of her subject in order to be a good leader, she must also have influence over her students, be well prepared to teach by staying ahead of them and provide them guidance by being a conduit. Likewise, effective CEOs, Presidents and Prime Ministers are visionaries who operate several steps ahead of the people they lead, are influential by getting them to carry out directives, and provide a paradigm for their subordinates to follow.

When looking for outstanding leaders, one may do well to scan the "endangered species" list. Quality leaders willing to take up the challenge to lead through thick-and-thin are few-and-far-between. Many start well but lose their resolve along the way. And instead of being duly rewarded, leadership turns out to be a thankless job, riddled with finger-pointing, and besieged by criticism. But leadership is a necessity; it's not a luxury. Leaders are those who provide guidance to the group. They stabilize the whole operation.

Leaders are the ones who dream the dreams. Leaders are the ones who are visionaries. They are the ones that have to answer the hardest questions within the outfit. They deal with the most complicated of issues. There is both risk and exhilaration in the full view that they have in mind, for they are the ones that are out front and continually address the perspective, where we are going (Swindoll, p. 333).

Non-leadership should not be an option for dads; being a reliable guide is a necessity to the fatherhood fraternity. Dads don't get to delegate that responsibility to someone else. The stork didn't air-deliver Junior and Princess, they're his. They have been entrusted with the privilege of giving sophistication to their naïve upstarts. Because a quick rendezvous in the sack can produce a child doesn't minimize the significance of fatherhood. At the risk of overstating the obvious, biologically fathering anyone is easy (stray dogs do it all the time), but steering the child to the threshold of adulthood is dad's true calling. It is his opportunity to fashion a fine legacy with them.

Of course, providing proper leadership to children presents its own peculiar challenge. Dad must sift through the mob of voices in his head and come up with a mentoring method tailor-made to his kids' unique design—one that will set them up for life success. An understanding of fatherly leadership goes a long way in helping men to be good mentors to their kids. How dad leads may determine how his kids face life's challenges. A fitting leadership approach must be used if father is to be successful in mentoring his children to thrive in an increasingly complex and competitive world.

The Uniqueness Of Fatherly Leadership

I've often wondered what goes through the minds of new fathers when they hold their babies in their arms for the very first time. What effect does cradling their tiny tots in their rugged, masculine, arms have upon them? Do any particular feelings come over them? Do they look into the eyes of little "chip-off-the-old-block" and say to themselves, 'ah my little devil you're going to grow up to be a notorious drug dealer, a feared criminal, or a prostitute?' I think not! That millions do grow up to lead dangerous, sad, or unfulfilled lives is an undeniable reality. I'd be willing to bet that they more than likely say to themselves, "My precious little angel, I am going to take good care of you. No amount of sacrifice is too great for me to secure your protection and happiness." And maybe they feel the weight of responsibility bearing down upon them to provide and care for their precious little innocent darling. Many fathers have reported that something special happened to them the moment they took their babies in their arms and looked into their squinting eyes for the first time. This is the time, we're told, some men finally grow up as they resolve to truly settle down and care for their helpless and needy offspring. "I can't think only of myself anymore; I have Princess to think about now."

While leadership may be the linchpin of many important ventures, fatherly leadership embodies a unique calling. This is because it distinguishes itself by the natural ties father has with his child; he's awakened by a compelling paternal affection for his vulnerable offspring clamoring for love and guidance. Fatherhood creates a bond which may be broken only in death—if even death can prevent dads from deeply caring and protecting the memory, name, and honor of their pride and joy. This deep-seated paternal affection isn't one-sided, it's reciprocal. A child's admiration and awe for his dad tends to be innate and almost indestructible. This was evident in the words of both a former United States president and a Hollywood actress.

During a farewell speech to his White House staff, President Richard Nixon remembered his father. He took a moment to recite his father's career failures. And then Nixon paused and said: "But he was a great man." When actress Angelica Huston was questioned about her father John Huston, she said, "... He was just bigger and better than anyone else."

It is easy to agree with Victor Parachin (2010) writing in *Vibrant Life* who pinpointed the connection between a father and his child when he wrote:

> Whether a father becomes successful or not, he is still a "great" man to his child and "bigger and better than anyone else." For a child a father is a combination of hero, guide, mentor, protector, teacher, and friend.

It is this larger-than-life quality I personally noticed in the eyes and voices of my boyhood friends when they spoke in glowing terms about their "can-do-no-wrong" fathers. This awe-filled awareness confirmed in me the truth of the proverb, "The glory of children are their fathers." This heroic characteristic fills children's hearts and inspires them to emulate their dads—boy, did I envy them!

This is not so with many other leadership arrangements. Heads of States, and CEOs who head up billion dollar corporations, as noble and honorable as those leadership ventures may be, they do not come with the proverbial umbilical cord connected to them. Little Junior has inherited dad's genes, his resemblance, smile, quirky antics, and is innocent. A strong sense of belonging is embedded in his mind. An unexplainable, deep, spiritual connection is undeniably at the core of the relationship to which dad feels naturally compelled to honor. Some fathers feel overwhelmed with the great responsibility they've inherited while others feel emotionally unprepared to deal with their new found love. But admittedly the new father may be clueless and, if the truth be told, scared. How is he going to do as a father? The forces working against him are many. Too often one of two extreme leadership styles emerges.

Consider this interesting depiction of the two leadership styles fathers tend to adopt. It is from *Aesop's Fables* and is titled, *The Frogs Who Wanted A King* by Rob John:

The frogs wanted a leader so they bothered Jupiter until he tossed them a log into the pond. And for a while, they were happy with their new log leader. But they soon found out they could jump up and down on their new leader and run all over him. He didn't resist or respond. That log didn't have any vision, direction, or purpose in his behavior, but just floated back and forth in the pond. This frustrated the frogs, who were really sincere about wanting "strong leadership."

They went back to Jupiter, complained about their log leader, and appealed for much stronger administration and oversight. Because Jupiter was weary of the complaining frogs, he gave them a stork, which stood tall above the members of the group and certainly had the appearance of a leader. The frogs were quite happy with their new leader. This leader stalked around the pond attracting great attention. Their joy turned to sorrow and ultimately to panic, for in a very short time the stork turned on them and began to eat its subordinates (Hewett, 1988, p. 313).

These two contrasting styles show how dad's approach to fatherly leadership affects his children's quality of life. The operative word here is the *how* of leadership. How will he handle himself in this role?

Terrors Of Tyrannical Leadership

Largely because of the prevailing male dominant model in society, many fathers perceive themselves king of their castle. And although strides have been made to take the edge off this skewed understanding of male leadership, there is still the perception by some that a heavy-handed, bossy, and domineering approach to leading is the way to go. Not unlike the stork in the story above, this approach to leadership incites fear and intimidation into children and can hurt their chances to blossom into their best selves. The autocrat is a tyrant, dictator, and despot who has crowned himself supreme ruler; he is one whose word is law and therefore must not be questioned.

Michael Jackson had been known to say, "I was a veteran before I was a teenager." Referring to his rigid schedule of rehearsing with his famous musical brothers, the beloved entertainer lamented the heavy-handed approach to leadership his father enforced. One of the great tragedies the King of Pop endured despite his phenomenal success was that he might have been deprived of a normal childhood. When he may have been making friends and playing, he was taken up with long hours of rehearsing his parts, or doing homework. Admittedly, to be good at anything requires a substantial investment of time spent practicing the task; but there is also such a thing as overkill. Those normal things kids everywhere do at certain stages of their development were denied him; instead, he lived under the constant threat of physical abuse from a well-meaning but unrelenting father obsessed with success. Michael later admitted that he was afraid of his father. Maya Angelou, who composed a piece called *We Had Him* and delivered it before loved ones at his funeral service, wrote "… his life was sheathed in mother love, family love, and survived and did more than that." Of course, father love was glaringly missing from her pen. Regardless of how hard "the gloved one" tried to recapture those childhood days later on in life, they forever eluded him. No toy was captivating enough to satisfy those lost moments. No later friendships could ever recapture what he missed during those particular times as a youth. Although he loved his dad, he never quite felt he could go to him to have a heart to heart talk. One wonders if the likes of his private amusement park, *Neverland* and his deep affection for children also reflected his need to relive parts of his youth which were denied him.

This kind of leadership will hardly be part of a healthy and happy family. Children are novices and prone to mistakes, forgetfulness, and trial-and-error learning. A tyrant isn't sensitive to these realities; he's forgotten that many people cut him slack and allowed him room to develop when he was younger.

A friend of mine knew I was exploring the topic of fatherly influence and told me about a story he'd heard. As I remember it, a father was passing by his daughter's bedroom and saw an envelope leaning against the pillow addressed to him. Thinking the worst, with trembling hands, increased heart rate, and a cold shiver slithering down his spine, he opened the letter which read:

Dear Dad, I am sorry to have to write to you this way. I want you to know that I ran away with my new boyfriend, because I didn't want to have any arguments with Mom and you. I have found real love with Rex. He is very nice, but I knew you would not like him because of all his tattoos, torn jeans, and leathers. Oh, I almost forgot, I am pregnant too. We're thinking of calling him Rex Jr. if it's a boy and Jennifer after Mom if it's a girl. We want to have lots more children. But don't worry about us. Rex said we will be very happy together. Do you know he owns a log cabin in the woods? Rex said that marijuana isn't as big a deal as people make it. He has been smoking "Pot" since he was thirteen. He is forty five now and nothing has happened to him except the time he had a bad dream about snakes and devils coming to get him. But it was only a dream. We plan on growing it ourselves and exchanging it with some of his friends for cocaine. But don't worry about me, remember I'm a grown woman now, I turn fourteen next month and I know how to handle myself. P.S.—Of course, none of this is really true. I'm over at Karen's house. I just wanted to remind you that there are worse things in life than my grade report on the kitchen table. Please let me know when it is safe to come home.

Kids need greater amounts of leniency and understanding from a firm but tenderhearted father who allows his children "wiggle room" in his fathering rule book. Fathers should keep in mind that leadership in the home doesn't equate to bossiness. Depending on how some fathers were raised and what they were exposed to, they may have confused the two.

> A boss creates fear; a leader creates confidence. Bossism creates resentment; leadership breathes enthusiasm. A boss says, "I"; a leader says, "We." A boss fixes blame; a leader fixes mistakes. A boss knows how; a leader shows how. Bossism makes work drudgery; leadership makes work interesting. A boss relies on authority; a leader relies on cooperation. A boss drives; a leader leads (Hewett, p. 312).

The difference is clear; bosses boss and leaders lead. Bossiness is all about one person, the boss. It is about the inflated ego and insatiable arrogance of the father who somehow misunderstood his position as leader. Leadership is all about the other. It's never about the individual except as one of the others. It is about influencing them through inspiration, instilling confidence, believing in them, encouraging them and being willing to show them how it's done not merely telling them how it's done.

Many have frowned upon the insensitivities of the tyrannical style of leadership in its many manifestations at various levels— the state level, institutional level, the corporate level and at the level of the home. The women's liberation movement in particular brought these issues to the public's consciousness by speaking out and protesting against them. *Child Protective Services* and human rights groups chimed in by passing and enforcing laws in favor of protecting minors. But in attempting to reverse generations of wrongs and adjust to a prescribed type of leadership, the pendulum seems to have swung to the other extreme.

Perils Of Passive Leadership

Instead of tyrannical leadership, many men overcompensated and became passive leaders. And while there is nothing attractive about the tyrannical leader, the inability to lead is just as loathsome and as much destructive to the mind of a child. The Duke of Windsor noticed this submissive parental tendency on one of his visits to America and sarcastically reported, "The thing that impresses me most about America, is the way the parents obey their children" (Hendricks and Phillips, p86). It has been said that nothing annoys the average child today like a disobedient parent. In many homes, the natural order has turned upside down. Children aren't supposed to occupy the position of control by manipulating their parents; they're supposed to comply. A family with either a despotic or spineless leader is dysfunctional at its very core.

"The father of five children won a toy from a raffle. He asked his kids who should get the toy. 'Who is the most obedient?' 'Who never talks back to mommy?' 'Who does everything she says?' Five small voices answered in unison, 'you play with it Daddy'" (Hewett, p. 199)! This father developed a reputation, even among his own little kids, for being the most obedient to their mother. He was most compliant and never talked back; he did everything she said. Being a proper leader doesn't amount to going along with everything the wife says. Of course many husbands found that if they wanted peace in the home, contradicting and disagreeing with their wives didn't help their cause. But this arrangement is neither a remedy for the tyrannical approach to leadership nor is it honorable behavior. No woman respects a man who doesn't know how to lead, take a stand, or who lacks backbone. Even the most independent woman appreciates a man who knows what he wants, and isn't afraid to contradict her. And although the children enjoy getting away with murder from their weak fathers, they usually grow up with a host of maladjustments to authority and leadership. Like the frogs they may, for a while, be happy jumping up and down on such a leader. They may run all over him especially when he offers neither resistance nor response. But it wouldn't be long before all involved figure out he has no direction or purpose to his behavior except to float back and forth in the house. This situation will surely lead to chaos.

A sheriff's office distributed a list of rules titled *How to Raise a Juvenile Delinquent in Your Own Family*. The list strikingly resembled that of the passive leader:

> Begin with infancy to give the child everything he wants. This will insure his believing that the world owes him a living. Pick up everything he leaves lying around. This will teach him he can always throw off responsibility to others. Take his part against neighbors, teachers, and policemen. They are all prejudiced against your child. He is a "free spirit" and never wrong. Finally, prepare yourself for a life of grief. You're going to have it (Hewett, p.194).

Fatherly leadership is too important to the maturation of our young to adopt the tyrannical approach or succumb to the deceptiveness of the passive posture. Neither of those methods is a good fit for the successful father. A more balanced leadership style should be pursued.

Sensitivities Of Servant-Leadership

Because we're mentoring the young and naive in the art of skillful living, it is essential that dad covers all his bases by adopting a complete approach. It is only natural that children look to their parents for leadership. The young want to make sense of the confusing world they have been brought into. Dad's rugged physical appearance, his deep baritone voice, his manly stance, his sense of frankness and certainty all communicate to Junior and Princess that he knows the way. And for a while, they will follow him whether he's a good or bad leader. Trust in the dad is developed from the earliest stages of the infant's journey. From the child's perspective, this may happen simply because his daddy is providing and caring for him. From the father's standpoint, a bond based on affection may be established simply because the child is his descendent. Dad's caring, coupled with an undeniable sense of responsibility, allow him to employ a balanced approach to mentoring his child. This natural paternal affection is also the ingredient responsible for influencing dad's style of leadership. The home is neither an army wherein tyrannical rule may be employed; nor is it a cruise ship to be passively placed on autopilot in calm waters when the way seems clear.

A fatherly leadership style incorporating both firmness and sensitivity wrapped up in the reassurance of love is likely to develop balanced individuals prepared for anything life throws at them. This style fits that of the servant-leader. Paradoxically, the two terms servant and leader are not polarized but coexist within the same individual to create someone who leads with a servant's heart. The concept may have roots in the basic proverb which says, "He who has not served knows not how to command." The emphasis here is on *how* to lead, not on the command. How refers to the manner: considerate, patient, understanding, tender, firm, and decisive. To him, maturity entails moving from a soft skin and tough heart to a tough skin and a soft heart because this is the apt combination needed for excellent leadership. He is not one who drives his kids with a bossy, tyrannical spirit. The servant-leader leads. He neither abdicates his position nor does he lord it over his children; instead, he leads with an attitude of service (although not servitude) to them. The servant-leader leads by example. He does not ask his kids to do anything, or go anyplace he is not first willing to do or go. The servant-leader maintains an open door policy with his kids. He does not view his word as law in the sense that they cannot even ask a question or express their views and feelings on any matter. He understands that the best way to succeed in his task of leadership requires encouraging open dialogue, not by cutting them off. He is keenly aware that he cannot treat each of his children the same but according to their peculiar personalities, level of understanding, and needs. When shopping around for an effective way to mentor and guide his precious descendents, he selects firmness over either roughness or cowardice. He employs tact when he must deal with sensitive and difficult issues. He is quick to admit when he was wrong, and he understands that this doesn't cast him as a weakling in his children's eyes; but, establishes his strength in their minds and provides grounds for openness, trust, and honesty. The servant-leader is transparent. He's an open book. But he understands that he needs to maintain a role distinction between himself and his children—that they're not buddies. He lives his role and grooms his young in their role. He finds agreement with Henry Ford, "A good leader inspires others to have confidence in him; but a great leader inspires them with confidence in themselves" (Hendricks and Phillips, p. 201). He is willing to sacrifice all to ensure the safety, comfort, peace, happiness, and overall wellbeing of his family. This is why the essential ingredient that makes fatherly leadership different from other leadership ventures is affection.

The story is told about the time famous New York diamond dealer Harry Winston found out that a wealthy Dutch businessman was interested in a particular type of diamond. Winston wasted little time to contact the Dutchman and invited him to his store to view the precious stone. Upon the collector's arrival at the store, a highly knowledgeable salesman was assigned to show him the diamond. Knowing the importance of the client, the salesman meticulously presented every important feature and was careful to point out the fine details of the precious stone. The Dutchman praised the jewel but kindly declined to purchase it, signifying that it wasn't quite what he has looking for. From a distance, Winston observed the sales pitch. He intercepted the collector, who began to make his way to the door, and requested a second opportunity to show him the diamond. The high profile customer consented. The jeweler then showed him the same stone choosing instead to focus on his genuine admiration for the item and the rarity of its kind. Instantly the merchant had a change of heart and decided to purchase the diamond. In the moments following the purchase while it was still being packaged, the customer curiously asked the jeweler, "What made me buy it the second time?" Winston's reply was that although the salesman is very knowledgeable about diamonds and is paid a competitive salary, he lacks an important ingredient. He went on to say that he would be happy to double the salesman's pay if he could put into him what he lacks. "He *knows* his diamonds, but I *love* them" (LeBoeuf, 1989). Servant leaders lead based on the principle of affection. Being careful to do everything right, dot all "Is" and cross all "Ts", without the most important ingredient "affection," signals to them that we don't care. They rightly believe that some other motive is driving our behavior towards them. We must show that we care; they need to know that we care. Leading them through serving them sends that message.

Of course, children are much more precious than diamonds. This is the secret ingredient without which the leadership fathers provide will be drudgery and an uphill struggle. Love and affection makes everything better. It was William Shakespeare who said that love's best habit is a soothing tongue. It softens harsh words, puts out fires of burning anger, and forgives trespasses. That natural paternal affection is indispensible to the whole venture's success. During the hum-drum of everyday life, there are times when fathers' love for their forgetful, error-prone kids will be put to the test. But his affection for them will keep him committed to the rewarding task of fatherhood.

It is said that you don't get a second chance at a first impression. Of greater consequence is the one opportunity to shape the lives of our young. No second opportunities are granted to undo the damage created by bad leadership. Any dent on the soul, hurt to the heart, scar on the spirit, any tear on the psyche, whether intentionally or unintentionally tends to leave deep and lasting wounds. The following confession comes from a heavy-hearted father who thought money, nice things, and glossing over problems to keep the peace was the way to father until he realized he got matters wrong. But he's not alone, these are common misunderstandings committed by many dads. From a piece called *A Father's Prayer of Enlightenment,* John Ellis after addressing his heavenly father, lamented:

Winston "Terry" Sutherland, PhD

I didn't realize that all it takes is my love...

> I thought that all I had to do to be a father
> was make money, stay at home and supply all their
> material needs. All I taught them was that there
> is more to being a dad. The problem is they will
> have to guess what being a dad really is (Gray,
> 1996, p. 117).

Although there isn't much we can do to turn back the hands of time to redo incidents we could've handled better (you cannot rebottle spilled milk), it may not be too late to rebuild with the ones we have caused pain. No father is perfect. None has all the answers. All dads can look back at various situations they wish they managed better. Thankfully, life affords opportunities to admit short-comings, seek forgiveness, and mend relationships. Wise fathers seize those opportunities and prevent them from festering. They haven't developed a politician's aversion to the words "I'm sorry." They're quick to humble themselves and seek to repair broken relationships.

Here are a few universally recognized traits of good leadership which bears directly upon dad's leadership influence.

It makes sense that if someone is going to lead he should know the way. Good leaders tend to have a *vision*. They see the big picture and know where they're heading. Every father should have some picture in his mind as to where he wants his family to be. He should envision what he ultimately wants his family to become. This vision needs to be shared with his wife. She ought to know and be on board with where they are heading. Shortsighted dads might be compared to the caterpillar pointing to a butterfly which just flew overhead, saying to another caterpillar, "You can't get me up in one of those things for a million dollars." They can't seem to see their way past their current situations. But even the longest night is followed by the morning. Current circumstances will eventually pass.

Resourceful leaders win the respect of their children. It is one thing to know where you want to go but it is quite another thing to be able to get there when the time comes. I came across a useful quote which says, "It matters not what you can do; if you cannot do it when it matters." It is important to actually have the means to get where you're going. Resourcefulness separates the men from the boys; the doers from mere dreamers and talkers. Unfortunately some men seem to have acquired a reputation for being poor at this. It has been said "if you want to get something said, ask a man; but, if you want to get something done, ask a woman." Fathers, you'll agree, we need to remedy this. Resourceful leaders find solutions in the face of mounting challenges. They don't make excuses even with sincere and genuine setbacks. They understand that people are depending upon them and that they need to deliver for the benefit of all.

Good leaders live by *integrity*. They understand that if they cannot be relied upon, the people they lead will not trust them. They know it is important to honor their word and keep promises and appointments. They mean what they say and say what they mean. Leaders, who've built a reputation for breaking promises, learn that there will be little or no faith placed in them. Such leaders aren't taken seriously by their kids or anyone for very long.

Effective leaders have found it important to be *approachable*. Embedded in dad's influence of affection is his desire to be considerate and understanding. These loving father-leaders keep the lines of communication open so they may be reached and their kids may feel welcomed when approaching them at any time. I believe it was Maya Angelou who said, "People will forget what you said, people will forget what you did, but people will never forget how you made them feel." How true. Kids know when they're not welcome and they form deep impressions about being shunned. Formality, rigidity, erecting barriers to being approached, is a full-proof way to discourage closeness with your kids.

This inviting and accommodating atmosphere is also akin to the "*happiness* factor" fathers would do well to cultivate. Although each individual is responsible for his own happiness, father as a leader occupies that strategic position to greatly influence his children's joy. An unhappy family reflects directly upon the leader of the home. So if Honey and the kids are unhappy, all eyes will be upon daddy. While this may seem unfair, there is something to be said for the leader setting the atmosphere in his home. Of course this does not mean that he has to comply with every whim and fancy of his wife and kids. But good leaders tend to create a climate whereby threats to the happiness of their families are quickly diffused. And a proactive approach inclusive of fostering cheerfulness may be a good offensive tactic. Effective dads encourage lots of laughter and gladness—they are mindful they're leading families not businesses or troops.

Everything rises and falls with the leadership. That's why great fathers strive to be the best they can be for their kids. Whether or not they received any mentoring from their own fathers, good dads find a way to be the leaders they ought to be. Getting this right means paving the way for a long and delightful relationship with his children because the proper ingredients have been put in place. He may then harvest the benefit of watching his kids go on to lead wholesome and constructive lives. There is no greater joy than the satisfaction a man has from knowing he has mentored his children and is now able to observe them live with dignity and honor. Dad's influence of affection is key to the lasting legacy he desires to leave; it unlocks the heart's doors of those whom he cherishes most. It is the secret to the happiness of the family and to the greatest joys we could hope for as fathers.

Chapter 5

Dad's Influence of Association: *Being Present*

Ninety percent of life is just showing up.
—Woody Allen

A Traveling Dad's Dilemma

Harry Chapin sang the heart-melting, tear-jerker *Cats In The Cradle* about his son Josh. Adored by millions, this song tells the story of a traveling dad whose life became busy to the point of threatening his closest relationships. In a masterstroke of songwriting Chapin, like a tour guide, walks his audience through this sad reality plaguing many hard working dads. Unsurprisingly, we find ourselves choked-up by the longing of this bright-eyed little boy whose adoring wishes were simply to spend time with his dad and grow up to be just like him. Beginning with his son's uneventful birth, Chapin found himself torn between his career responsibilities and his family duties. "There were planes to catch and bills to pay." He tried justifying his busy lifestyle while simultaneously lamenting the simple joys he was missing out on. With the bittersweet refrain of his lonesome son vowing to be like him, for many, Chapin's words convey an eerie familiarity. The irony was that as the years went by, the tables had turned; the roles switched. Chapin eventually retired and longed to spend time with his son while Josh grew up to be a man and finally got his wish; he became just like his dad—too busy to "hang-out" with him.

On one occasion before Chapin performed this musical poetry he confessed to his audience, "It's about my boy, Josh." Then admitted, "And frankly it scares me to death!" Here are the lyrics to the opening lines of *Cats In The Cradle*:

> My child arrived just the other day
> He came to the world in the usual way
> But there were planes to catch and bills to pay
> He learned to walk while I was away
> —Harry Chapin

Like many well intentioned and hard working fathers who adore their little boys and girls, Chapin had genuine work responsibilities which kept him away from home. You don't get the impression he was off womanizing, boozing, gambling, or purposely avoiding his domestic responsibilities as a father. After all, "there were planes to catch and bills to pay." He was a musician and a recording artist. This particular ditty went all the way to number one on the popular charts. Singing was his skill, his job, by which he put food on the table and a place for them to call "home." How else will Junior and Princess be provided for? But the singer still seemed to express a measure of remorse whenever he sang this song. Could it be a sense of guilt or the fear of resentment being expressed as he thought of his son's innocent and needy smile which never dimmed every time he said goodbye to him? Or, might it be a father's "gut-feeling" that by his absence he was letting him down? Maybe it was the notion that somehow he was setting up his son for a lifetime of struggle—making him vulnerable to deficiencies common among kids of absentee fathers? Or it may simply be that he was going to miss him. Whichever it was, his reasons for expressing remorse weren't provided; but no father needs to have it spelled out to him, traveling dads live with contradictions tugging at their hearts. They grapple with striking the right balance between providing for their family and being around more.

Effects Of Father Absence

Although not all children of absentee and uninvolved fathers turn out the same, statistics on fatherless children paint a grim picture and tell an uninspiring story. Decedents of "rolling stone" dads have been the subject of untold studies and belong to an unenviable fraternity. Some reading the following statistics for the first time may be surprised to discover the sheer amount of problems associated with fatherlessness and negative emotions may be provoked. It's been reported that:

90% of homeless and runaway children are from fatherless homes [US D.H.H.S., Bureau of the Census].

80% of rapists motivated with displaced anger come from fatherless homes [Criminal Justice & amp; Behavior, Vol. 14, pp. 403-26, 1978].

71% of pregnant teenagers lack a father [U.S. Department of Health and Human Services press release, Friday, March 26, 1999].

63% of youth suicides are from fatherless homes [US D.H.H.S., Bureau of the Census].

85% of children who exhibit behavioral disorders come from fatherless homes [Center for Disease Control].

90% of adolescent repeat arsonists live with only their mother [Wray Herbert, "Dousing the Kindlers," Psychology Today, January, 1985, p. 28].

71% of high school dropouts come from fatherless homes [National Principals Association Report on the State of High Schools].

75% of adolescent patients in chemical abuse centers come from fatherless homes [Rainbows for all God's Children].

70% of juveniles in state operated institutions have no father [US Department of Justice, Special Report, September 1988].

85% of youths in prisons grew up in a fatherless home [Fulton County Georgia jail populations, Texas Department of Corrections, 1992].

Fatherless boys and girls are: twice as likely to drop out of high school; twice as likely to end up in jail; four times more likely to need help for emotional or behavioral problems. [US D.H.H.S. news release, March 26, 1999] (Retrieved 04/07/12 http://fatherhoodfactor.com/statistics).

Increases in births to unmarried women are among the many changes in American society that have affected family structure and the economic security of children. Children of unmarried mothers are at higher risks of adverse birth outcomes such as low birth weight and infant mortality than are children of married mothers [National Center for Health Statistics].

Can these be mere coincidences?

My reporting of these data isn't meant to be accusatory or merely to dwell upon the negatives; but to raise awareness about the many behavioral issues linked to fatherlessness. And the bad news is made worse with the last statistic reported by the National Center for Health Statistics, which refers to the trend in society of increased births to unmarried women. This affects family structure, economic security, and higher risks of infant deaths. There is no one-size-fits-all solution except fundamentally to start with being physically and emotionally present in our children's lives.

One of the root effects of father-absence in kids is the assumption some make that their fathers have rejected them. In the privacy of their inner thoughts they come to the conclusion that, "My father doesn't want me, obviously I must be bad, defective, or in some way unlovable." Of course, that line of thinking has little to do with the truth. Father-absence occurs for various reasons: inability to get along with their child's mother; some feel inadequate to bear the responsibility of raising a child; some haven't matured yet and are still thinking of themselves first; and the list of reasons is long. This subconscious feeling of rejection, destroys kids' self-esteem, saps their confidence, and overall gives them the feeling of inadequacy.

Also, children who grew up in father-absent homes have never had the opportunity to benefit from a man's take on life. They had no chance, for instance, to observe how their fathers would deal with a whole host of issues. From difficult concerns faced on a daily basis to trivial matters encountered moment by moment, fatherless kids aren't exposed to dad's approach. If Henry Ward Beecher was right that, "The most important thing a father can do for his children is to love their mother," then his absence robs them of a big part of their development. Kids need to know, what intimacy looks like in a man. Is it true that men aren't supposed to cry? What does he do in lieu of accessing his emotions and letting the pain out? They were robbed of the opportunity to see how dad handled conflicts between himself and their mother, which could be some of his most challenging battles. As Muhammad Ali once said, "My toughest fight was with my first wife." This may be surprising coming from a man who battled the likes of Joe Frazier and George Foreman in the boxing ring. So when Junior marries the girl of his dreams and conflicts arise between them, he has no ingrained model from which to begin, no reference point to go back to. He'll have to learn how to fight his toughest fights by trial and error. He had no father to admit to him, after he cools off let's say, that he may or may not have handled the situation well and what he may have done differently. These kids were deprived of observing how dad would have dealt with threats to his home from rival men. The amount of intangibles kids are deprived of is innumerable.

Effects Of Father Presence

When a man on his deathbed is asked what he'd do differently, he never wishes he made more money or acquired more things; instead, he talks about how much he wished he spent more time with his family. Neglect of those primary relationships are what fathers often express the most regret about, especially failing to spend enough time with them. That's what really matters, not the things which seem to occupy us and consume most of our time. Long time *NBC* and *Los Angeles Times* reporter, Cal Thomas (1985) expressed the sentiments of some when he wrote:

> As a reporter for twenty-one years, I have known five Presidents, traveled through much of the world, had the heady experience of being asked for my autograph, and enjoyed the praise of a small number of people. None of that meant as much as the hugs and kisses I have received from my children (and wife!) and the voluntary acknowledgments of their love for me.

Pursuing personal glory, when finally achieved, can leave us disappointed and unfulfilled. The interesting thing is, when we're younger and healthy, we don't seem to understand this. It's when we are more mature and have acquired wisdom from years of experience that many come to similar conclusions. Trivial things seem so much more important at the time. But to be fair, not everybody takes a lifetime to realize this; some seem blessed with the wisdom of the ages while still young. These are the ones who build a legacy with their kids. These are the fathers who can look their sons and daughters in the eyes at graduations and weddings with a sense of deep satisfaction that they built a strong relationship with them. They realize that it is there, in the midst of this amazing gift called fatherhood that the fulfillment of a happy life may be attained.

This belief is echoed in the voices of those who participated in the *Survey of Fatherly Influence*. In more than one category, over and over again, as sure as the day follows the night, many people overwhelmingly said that:

a) Their favorite memories of their father had something to do with *spending time with him,*

b) What they would recommend father and son do together to build a bond was to *spend time with each other,* not send them away or just tell them what to do,

c) Part of their role as father was to *spend time with their children,* and

d) The advice they would offer new fathers is to *spend time with their children.*

Spending time appeared to be the number one advice offered to dads to positively influence their children. What was not said may have been even more telling. No one advised dads to buy more things for their kids, give them more money, or be sure to have an attractive home for them or any such thing. It was unanimous, even by its absence that no amount of money or material things could substitute for quality time and being physically present. No price may be placed on the value of a man's physical presence to the health and happiness of his children.

The Power Of Presence

The importance of a man's presence to the mentoring relationship is not a new trend; it predates all of these reports by thousands of years. The necessity of fathers spending quality time with their children isn't some discovery by our planet's brightest minds and passed on as mushy, psychobabble as some would suggest. Being physically present has always been crucial to the mentoring of the naïve, to the preparing of the unprepared. It has always been critical to building into the lives of loved ones in a meaningful way.

Take, for instance, the emphasis placed on being physically present in a two thousand year old narrative. Of all the things that may be said about Jesus, one thing is undeniable—His historical existence, His physical presence. That He lived and walked the dusty streets of Mesopotamia may be verified through both secular and biblical records as they document His life, family history, words, and deeds. The manner by which He "showed-up" provides us insight into the importance of "being there."

To accomplish His purposes, He decided upon a plan that would leave a lasting legacy—one that sent ripples down to our present time. Mentoring fathers essentially do the same, building into their children, and leaving a lasting legacy. They pass on their years of accumulated "know-how" to their kids who in turn add their own accumulated knowledge and, in turn, pass it on to their children. This marathon relay can go on for generations as the mentoring baton is passed down from father to child. The ancient Chinese believed: if your vision is for a year, plant wheat; if your vision is for a decade, plant trees; if your vision is for a lifetime, plant people. Mentoring is all about planting and cultivating people. Jesus' plan was simple. He would mentor.

The fundamental message of this book is that fathers mentor their children; be more than a provider, affirm them, and guide them.

Jesus picked a small group of men to "be around" Him as an important part of His long-term mission. Mark wrote about it in his Gospel. "He [Jesus] selected twelve that they might be with Him." There it is, almost unnoticeable and easy to miss. Mark reports that He handpicked twelve protégés to be **with Him**. The rest of the statement said, "… and that He might send them out to proclaim." Now, doesn't being *with Him* seem a strange purpose? That is what the ancient record said He did; He chose twelve followers to be *with Him*. If you're like me, you'd be wondering what's so significant about being *with Him*? Weren't there other ways to get His ideas across to them? Couldn't He prepare a manifesto and pass it along to them? They could read it over and over and study it thoroughly until they really understood his message. Sure, the printing press wasn't invented yet, but He could have produced a written document and save Himself the trouble of spending all that time with them.

For one thing, being *with Him* created an atmosphere whereby His disciples could have observed His every move. Now, He orchestrated this on purpose; but, fathers have this choreographed naturally. Dads inherit their own disciples. This is necessary to the mentoring process. Some things are better caught than taught and "being around" maximizes the chances of catching valuable life lessons. Being physically present provides opportunities to take advantage of those teachable moments popping-up from time to time. Much of meaningful learning involves mimicry. Learners emulate their heroes and adapt their stellar habits to their own lifestyle. Moreover lasting life lessons are hardly ever scheduled; they are usually spontaneous and sometimes surprise us when we least expect them. Mentoring minded fathers recognize this and take full advantage of the natural ebbs and flow in life. They are often found doing things with their kids. Of course, mentoring fathers are motivated both, by their affection for their little ones, and by their kids' dependence upon them. This mutual interest allows for a wonderful reciprocity; for, no dad believes he deserves the hero worship his bright-eyed, innocent kid heaps upon him.

My high school biology teacher, Mr. Ramdeen, was fond of telling the class, "You can't get this stuff by osmosis you know, you have to go home and study." That's still funny after all these years. You'd remember that osmosis is the movement of fluid from a place of high concentration to a place of low concentration through a semi-permeable membrane. I mention this because there are some types of learning that may best be described as learning by osmosis. That hard to explain learning which comes from spending time *with* a mentor might be described as taking place through the process of osmosis—the movement of "knowhow and understanding" from a place of high concentration to a place of low concentration. Dad's presence is not optional to the mentoring process. The greatest impact is not made from a distance.

Another benefit of spending time with Him was that His followers saw how He lived. They were *with Him* and saw how He dealt with the Pharisees and Sadducees. They were *with Him* in the boat when He was sound asleep during a life-threatening storm. They were *with Him* when He fed five thousand followers with a kid's lunch. There were times when He did things in the crowds that His disciples didn't quite grasp. But when the crowds dwindled and dispersed to their homes, the curious from among the twelve questioned Him about those things. His disciples were able to observe, not only *what* He did but *how, why, with whom*, and *when* He did various things. Of course, they also picked up on the things He didn't do and the reasons associated with those omissions. They were *with Him* and observed how He managed the accusations regarding the woman taken in adultery. They couldn't forget how He rescued her from being stoned to death as the self-righteous, blood-thirsty religious leaders were demanding. These and countless other instances both recorded and unrecorded provided opportunities for deeply impacting those around Him.

Another hidden benefit resulting from dads spending quality time with their children may only come to the surface many years later as was evident in the impact Jesus' life had upon His men. This phenomenon may be observed in the simple practice common among marketers to persuade us that their products work; and that is exactly the point of this suggestion—mentoring and being physically present has transformative influence upon children's lives. The marketing technique in question is the "before-and-after" photo. The "Before" photo represents an unpolished condition prior to the application of the change-agent; and the "After" photo depicts the strength of the change-agent. It's about the makeup of the twelve. Who were they? How did they turn out as a result of the change-agent which, in this case was "being with Him"?

The Before

The composition of that enduring movement may come as a surprise to many. These twelve weren't necessarily your best and brightest; they were by-and-large quite ordinary. Some have referred to them as a rogue bunch. In fact, others have suggested that the team might be compared with the twelve deviants portrayed in the classic movie *The Dirty Dozen*. These were criminals who had been on prison's death row and given a chance at freedom if they accepted what may end up being a suicide mission. But although the comparison might be unfair, the twelve disciples were indeed a curious bunch. Consider this "rap sheet" on the chosen twelve.

Simon the zealot was a knife carrying gang member who vowed to kill Romans and Roman sympathizers. Judas Iscariot regularly pilfered money from the treasury. He is probably best known for betraying Jesus to His enemies for the price of a common slave, and shamefully took his own life by hanging. When someone is called a Judas he is essentially being referred to as a traitor. Even among gang members and common criminals, loyalty is sacred. Matthew was an embezzler of funds; he overcharged his own countrymen to pay his Roman bosses who were abusing his countrymen. One wonders how he and the zealot got along in the same camp. Peter, like Judas, committed the unthinkable when it comes to group code—he was disloyal. He turned his back on his mentor when He faced the most trying time of His earthly life, denying that he ever knew Him. James and John, nicknamed "the sons of thunder" because their father had an explosive temper, wanted to use their association with Jesus to call down fire from heaven to consume a city populated with innocent people. Thomas also earned the nickname, "Doubting Thomas" because of his infamous refusal to believe Jesus rose from the dead until he plunged his fingers through the nail prints in His hands and the wound in His side.

Not many would have selected the same twelve. Most of us would probably have looked for reputable people among the elite, with good family pedigree. But the more common they were, the greater the opportunity to demonstrate the power of mentoring. Their flaws magnified the chance to see the influence mentoring can have upon the most unpolished and deviant people. Their questionable character traits were collectively the perfect background against which to examine the power of the change-agent, "being *with Him.*" This is not unlike the black cloth used by jewelers who use it as background to the clear multi-angled diamond so they can better see the beauties of the precious stone. So the obvious question is: what impact, if any, did the change-agent of "being *with Him*" have upon these men?

The After

The disciples themselves would find it hard to believe that they became the established pillars who started out so unrefined. Each of them, with the exception of Judas, shed his timidity, cowardice, and mean-spiritedness. They adopted courage, gentleness, and unyielding faith. The spinelessness exhibited when they denied *being associated with* Jesus in the face of His imminent persecution, was replaced with their own determination to spread his message far and wide. History records that these same men later sacrificed their lives accepting martyrdom in defense of their association *with Him* and His message. Peter requested that he face his own crucifixion upside down because he felt unworthy to be crucified like his leader. The rest of the disciples likewise perished refusing to renounce their allegiance to the legacy of their mentor. Civil Rights icon and Nobel peace laureate Dr. Martin Luther King Jr. believed that people who haven't found something for which they're willing to die, haven't really begun to live. These eleven were willing to give their lives for the honor of being associated with a person in whom they came to believe. The presence of their change-agent had a profound influence upon them. Something life-changing happened between the time they met Jesus and the time He left them—mentoring happened. That time spent *with Him* made all the difference. It is essentially the influence of association. By being associated with an influential leader in their lives, the intangible virtues of character, values, courage, and faith, rubbed off on them. Associating with Him provided an atmosphere for easy transmission of ideas and learning in general—the powerful kind of learning most don't even realize is taking place.

Amazingly, of all the possible methods available to Jesus to launch a global movement that would stand the test of time, He chose mentoring. This is significant. He obviously thought the best way to impart His views would be by way of camaraderie. He took advantage of the proven evidences of apprenticeship and on-the-job training as His chosen method. His simple but effective method depended upon the impactful influence of association. Be present. Be around. Be there. By doing so, it will have great positive influences that will last for generations to come. It was His way to take advantage of those unscheduled, learning moments which surface during the natural course of life.

Once again we find that the need for a father's presence receives compelling support from ordinary Americans. According to the *Survey of Fatherly Influence*, thirty-seven percent of the participants were raised by only their mother, only two percent were raised by their fathers alone, and fifty-six percent had both parents contributing to their upbringing, leaving a void when it came to having a male father-figure in the home. The U. S. Census Bureau reported in 2010 that 23% of children in the United States lived only with their mother. The true percentage is believed to be higher since many people don't bother to fill out the survey and report their household status. This amounts to millions of fatherless children who had no fatherly guidance.

They have never benefitted from their dad's perspective on life issues. They missed out on having him say to them, "I love you," or "I'm proud of you," which when put together 90% of survey participants said they would most like to hear their fathers say to them. As a result, the fatherless will likely seek this affirmation elsewhere and not everyone from whom this is sought will have their interest at heart.

The Father Factor

But dad's influence of association is not limited to teachable moments and the lasting impact of a changed life. Within the formula of the family, a missing father is just that—a missing piece of the formula for a wholesome home, and by extension a wholesome child. Men are programmed in their masculinity to protect women and children. Dad's absence must not be overlooked, brushed aside, or dismissed as unimportant. We shouldn't think dad's disappearance leaves mom and siblings unscathed. His absence leaves a gaping need; it creates an unquenchable thirst. Many of our young are growing up with social, psychological, educational, and spiritual deficiencies resulting from the void left by dad's absence. Those who are least aware of their deficits may take longer to begin to address them. Many never face them at all. They may either have no explanation or misguided justifications for some of their erratic behaviors.

Erma Bombeck in her book, *Family—The Ties that Bind... and Gag!* Told of a little girl who didn't quite understand what fathers do. But she didn't have any confusion about what mothers do. According to Bombeck, this child didn't think that much about her dad until one morning when he didn't go to work but went to the hospital and died the following day. To her, he was just someone who left in the morning and was happy to see his family when he came home at night. He was the one who opened tight jars when no one else could. And when he cut himself shaving no one showed any excitement or kissed it. He was the one to take the pictures but was never in them. When it was raining he'd go out into the rain and bring the car to the front door for everyone to get in. When anyone was sick he went to get the medicine for them, that sort of thing. But she didn't quite know what his role was or how he fit into the family. Here is what she had to say.

> Whenever I played house, the mother doll had a lot to do. I never knew what to do with the daddy doll, so I had him say, "I'm going off to work now," and threw him under the bed. The funeral was in our living room and a lot of people came and brought all kinds of good food and cakes... I went to my room and felt under the bed for the daddy doll. When I found him, I dusted him off and put him on my bed. He never did anything. I didn't know his leaving would hurt so much (1988, p.2).

What's lacking when dad is absent from his children's lives whether he goes AWOL—Away WithOut Leave, MIA—Missing In Action, or is deceased? For one thing, mother is left to shoulder the burden of raising the children all by herself. She will attempt to meet that gaping need left by him, so she has to be both mother and father. She has to be provider, protector, nurturer, and exact discipline when needed. As a woman, she would have been expecting to be the recipient of these things, not the embodiment of them. In other words, she would like a provider and protector of her own. When she was looking for a spouse, one of her biggest needs was security; so, both provider and protector roles are now stretched for her and the children.

The statistics on fatherless children strongly imply that a father's presence in the home brings with it certain stabilizing factors. A father's presence provides protection from questionable men who view fatherless homes as easy targets. I'll never forget a conversation with prisoners some years ago. While part of a community group visiting local prisoners to conduct a "Men's Talk," one particular inmate recounted how his mother "got ripped off over and over again by mechanics and repairmen." He went on to say that as kids he and his little sister were "shushed" and pushed aside while some men "who appeared cool in the beginning" later turned out to be @$$#$ only to take advantage of mom and then disappear. A father's presence discourages that.

Former Navy Seal, Howard Watson, tells of a time a young man came by to take out his teenage daughter on a date. As he was taking the garbage to the roadside curb for sanitation pick up, a teenage boy around his daughter's age approached his front door. Now this kid showed up wearing "saggy" pants, constantly keeping a hand on to prevent it from sliding off him. His face was decorated with pieces of metal hardware piercing his nose, lips, tongue, eyebrows, and ears. Howard didn't quite know which upset him more; the notion of a stranger overlooking him in the driveway en route to knocking on his front door? Or, that this youth had the audacity to attempt taking out his princess looking the way he did. After getting his attention, Mr. Watson advised the suitor to get a belt for his pants, and remove the facial hardware if he wants to even be considered for a date with his little girl. When the former Navy Seal went inside he had to contend with the ire of his teenage sweetheart who accused him of being judgmental. She charged him with judging the guy based only on his appearance. Her father's defense to her accusation was, "If it looks like a duck, walks like a duck, and quacks like a duck, it's probably a duck!" Needless to say, daughter was irate. Some weeks later, she came running to him, threw her arms around him, kissed him, and thanked him for protecting her from the young man. One of her other friends went on a date with him and told her horrible stories about how he mistreated her.

Dads act as deterrents to unsuspecting threats. Father's presence is a force-field to unsuspecting and uncompromising forces. Of course, this does not deny that well dressed teenage boys also mistreat young ladies. But it emphasizes dad's ability to discern and to protect his family.

When we were younger, everybody in Junior High was afraid of the neighborhood bully. The only time you weren't afraid of him and his gang of goons was when your father or big brother was with you. As long as your father was present, you felt safe. So when caught alone, a simple reminder to the intimidating neighborhood bullies that "I'll tell my father" was enough to buy you a pass.

The perspective a father gives to his kids cannot be provided by their mother. No matter how wonderful a job she does raising them, she will never be a man. A mother's natural nurturing instinct to some issues raised in the home, for instance, may not always provide the necessary firmness a father finds natural to him. Both are needed of course. Likewise, a father can never be a woman and provide those things a mother naturally provides. Dad's absence leaves a void and throws off the balance a child needs.

When dad is absent, these areas of fatherly providence and protection are left wide open for imposters. Mother alone struggles to provide a balanced home. Here are some other things a father's presence provides.

A father's physical presence builds confidence in his children. Dad's presence in the home gives off the feeling of security. This leads to a sense of self-confidence. We all function best when we feel safe. Psychologically, his kids know that the protector is there. So, they're free to concentrate their energies and efforts on other matters. Both sons and daughters benefit greatly from this sense of male protection. But they do so in different ways according to their needs. Girls, aware that they cannot match boys for physical strength, benefit even more from dad's masculine presence in the home. Boys benefit through reinforcement. They can see what they may become.

Fathers instill in their children the importance of a strong work-ethic by developing in them a proper mindset toward work. The fatherless may struggle to understand the relationship between hard work and due reward. Both passive and absent fathers deprive their kids of this "game changer" in life. A strong work ethic is a game changer because it may be responsible for providing much of our human physical needs—food, clothing, shelter, pride, and confidence. Work is much more than money; it gives us a chance to explore our creative skills. It fills us with pride because we're producing something constructive. The children of absentee fathers may never put up with some of the challenges that come with a job. They may never outgrow the strong childhood thinking that life is supposed to cater to them. They run the risk of getting stuck in an unrealistic, immature set of expectations from society. It goes without saying that this can later destroy them and their loved ones.

Fathers help their children understand the importance of respecting authority. Dad instills respect for authority by helping his kids understand when they've crossed the line with them and their mother. While he, along with mom, gives both the spoken and unspoken rules for the household, it is usually the father who applies the proverbial "rod of correction to the seat of learning." Knowing the consequences of insubordination, fathers are especially attentive to their children's failure to respect their parents. Their male egos are heightened to respond to any challenges to their jurisdiction. Dads know kids can have run-ins with authority figures, especially the law; so, he moves swiftly to instill the fear of God in them.

One of the joys of fatherly mentoring manifests itself in the opportunity to help develop critical thinking skills. He may help them develop patient reasoning and teach them to use their minds like responsible adults. He may show them how to arrive at useful questions and the importance of producing meaningful answers. He may help them develop into leaders by not settling for half-baked answers but to question answers, question the status quo. In preparing Junior and Princess, dad will coach them to be a step ahead of everyone and to anticipate consequences. He may also teach them how to read people, and how to discern their gibberish (Stenson, 2012).

Naturally, having both parents in the home is preferred. Single parenting is difficult and what's worse, it scars children. The effects of fatherlessness upon children are indeed devastating. What would we do without the many mothers who've toughed it out. Countless mothers have stepped up and done a good job of providing love and taking care of their children against great odds.

But merely being physically present (although better than being absent) is not enough. Being committed to stay the course and not to abandon his kids is good, right, and proper; but that doesn't mean it's mission accomplished. It's a start in the right direction. Dad's influence of association provides a protective presence; but his presence is best utilized when accompanied with a commitment to be involved in his kid's lives.

Chapter 6

Dad's Influence of Attention: *Being Involved*

It is not the same to talk of bulls as to be in the bullring.

—Spanish Proverb

Value Of Attention

James Boswell, the famous biographer of Samuel Johnson, often talked about a special day in his childhood when his father took him fishing. James' father was usually busy with his responsibilities as a Scottish lord and ruled his family with an iron fist. But that day was fixed in James' mind. Anyone who knew him often heard him talk about the things his father taught him during the course of their fishing experience. After hearing of that particular excursion so many times, it occurred to somebody to check the journal that Boswell's father kept to determine what he wrote about that fishing trip. We know how James felt about it, but how did his dad feel about that memorable event his son fondly recalled over and over again? Turning to that date, the researcher found only one sentence entered: "Gone fishing today with my son; a day wasted."

The most memorable and meaningful day in James' life was, to his father, nothing more than a waste of his time. Could their opinions of that time spent going fishing together be any different? Amazingly, the impact it had upon James is not an isolated thing unique to types like James. Our little ones cherish those moments we devote to showing them how to throw a fishing line or talking with them about life issues. This show of love fills them with indescribable pride. And since the glory of children are their fathers, these are the types of things they boast to their friends about. These are the things that answer unasked questions about their place in father's heart. It was when I witnessed my Junior High classmates exude such pride in their fathers that my eyes were opened to the absence of similar experiences with my dad.

Preparing our young to take life by the horns requires a deeper level of involvement than that of the disengaged father. This is where mentoring fathers roll up their sleeves and get their hands dirty in the messy joy of fatherhood. This is where meaningful teaching, guiding, and coaching take place. It is here that the real difference seen in the mentored child is made.

Mentoring fathers do not leave the outcome of their children's life-readiness to chance; they purposefully involve themselves in Junior and Princess' lives. These dads know that nothing could replace lost time, especially during early and adolescent stages of their lifelong journey. They take interest in the things and places their kids like; they find a hobby to share with Junior and go places with him; they talk to him about himself and what is expected of him as a man. They do the same with their daughters and quickly learn that it is important to listen to her, and talk to her about her worth as a young woman and how men differ from women in thought and behavior.

The involved father mentors his children at a more intimate level than the passive, disengaged father who may be physically present but emotionally distant. Involved dads are readily accessible to their children; their kids are free to approach them with any issue. Because they neither make it awkward nor erect barriers, kids enjoy open access to dads' wealth of experience. They take advantage of his store of knowledge and avoid many of the mistakes they would have made without his guidance. Sure, they'll make mistakes of their own, but with a well-laid foundation, mistakes may be fewer and less serious. The following narrative highlights dads' influence of attention and the benefits of fathers' involvement in their children's lives.

Building Indestructible Bonds

Cuba Gooding Jr. portrayed the character "Trey" in the classic movie, *Boyz 'N' The Hood*. When Trey was about 10 years old, his mother took him to live with his dad having grown increasingly frustrated with him. But his father's neighborhood was known for its violence, high crime, gang warfare, and rampant illegal drug dealings. If ever a boy needed fatherly mentoring, Trey was that boy. In his world, a passive or absent father meant you were on the fast track to prison or death.

When the pre-teen was dropped off, his father "Furious," played by Laurence Fishburne immediately implemented his philosophy by preparing Trey to thrive in that urban jungle. It was clear that he subscribed to the approach which says, "The best defense is a strong offense." Right away, he began to apply his version of fatherly mentoring. He launched preventative attacks on two fronts—on youthful rebelliousness and on neighborhood threats upon his home. Furious kept Trey occupied with household responsibilities while his friends roamed the streets and got into trouble. Putting him to work, he handed him a garden rake to rake-up the leaves in the yard and later to sanitize the bathroom. Noticing that Trey didn't take kindly to his new responsibilities, Furious thought to explain the reason for his apparent hardness. "These responsibilities may seem harsh, but they will keep you alive and out of jail." His deep, firm, but unmistakably loving voice left little room for compromise.

It wasn't long before Trey reunited with old friends he met on previous visits to his dad and began to make South Central, Los Angeles his home. As the narrative progressed, there followed a series of scenes contrasting the violence and crime in the neighborhood with the police's indifference towards the area's bleak state-of-affairs. In contrast to those morbid scenes were depictions of Furious constantly coaching young Trey in life-lessons. As if to say, in the midst of turmoil and hopelessness, there may be hope after all. Or, despite the bleak surroundings, with fatherly guidance there can be a bright future. In Trey's new home, those scenes vividly conveyed a flicker of hope in the midst of a forlorn, urban wasteland.

The time came when Trey and his friends were in their late teens. Then the worst happened. When his childhood "homeboy" is gunned down by a rival gang, Trey and his cohorts vowed to avenge his blood. Now his father, Furious, felt compelled to keep a handgun for protection in that crime-ridden neighborhood. (I suppose it was sort of a "by any means necessary" measure to survive in that lawless concrete jungle. It was inevitable that at some point he would have to confront an armed robber.) He stumbles upon Trey tightening his grip around the weapon with a premeditative look in his eyes. Furious quickly talks him out of a bad decision to get involved with violence. But later, during the stillness of the night and under the cover of darkness, Trey's raging emotions eclipsed his good judgment. He sneaked out through his bedroom window and joined the rest of the gang in pursuit of revenge.

Let's think about this for a moment. Your ten year old boy comes to live with you in a troubled district. You spend the next eight years helping him navigate his way around the enticements and traps lurking behind every corner of teenage years. You provide all his needs—you protect him, coach him, build a father-son bond with him, teach him that it's sometimes okay for men to cry and now you're looking forward to sending him off to a university. His future looked bright and full of hope. As a father you are about to exhale because those thorny teenage years are almost behind you. Then one day he violates all good sense, jumps through the window, and aligns himself with troublemakers in a moment that could cost him his reputation, his freedom, or his life. And it's all out of your hands.

After Trey's exit through the window, the next few moments were tense and frightfully frustrating for Furious. Parents who love their children know all too well, the gripping feeling of fearing the worst—that hollow vacuum sensation when your stomach sort of collapses inside you, that thumping of the heart, that feeling of breathlessness and dryness of the throat. It is at this point in the movie that the true power of mentoring is tested. By the way, there comes a time when things of value are tested—systems, ideas, methods, and philosophies. From time to time, a friend of mine would say to me, "Make sure your formula works!" Of course he is referring to my life formula, my philosophy of life. This was one of those times for Furious.

He was about to find out if his fathering formula worked. Both his own resolve to steer clear of violence and his philosophy of fatherly mentoring were under examination. The next scene will be forever etched on every attentive viewer's mind. It is the climax of the entire narrative.

Furious finds himself at a loss for what to do next, and that was just the trouble, he could do nothing. He did all he could and it was in his son's hands to do what he thought was right. Dad had to trust that what he poured into that which he loved most in this world, his only son, will accomplish its intended purpose. That central guiding principle: "Train up a child in the way he should go, and when he is old he will not depart from it," was being put to the test.

At this point, Furious needed to carve out a moment of time to clear his head and think. He found himself slumping down into his chair—the weight of the crisis crashing down upon his shoulders. Two silver stress-balls atop his desk found their way into his hand. Staring into nothingness, he maneuvers them between his fingers swishing them around like a ballerina twirling her baton. The imagery was astounding; it mirrored the tensions converging in his mind, building and swirling around, thought grinding against thought, furiously searching for a sensible solution, a peaceful end.

But this was the moment of reckoning. All those times spent exposing, guiding, teaching, coaching, and mentoring Trey, will have to stand for something. Will he apply the "cost versus benefits" principle they went over so many times? And the inevitable questions, did he neglect to teach him something important? Had he done enough? Later that night, as the gang drove up and down the streets of the city, all good sense returned and settled Trey's turbulent emotions. It was clear to him now

Winston "Terry" Sutherland, PhD

that he didn't belong in that car on its way to the worst mistake of his life. He grew increasingly uncomfortable about the whole ordeal and eventually got out of that battle tank before it entered the war zone. He couldn't go through with it; he just couldn't do it. Something within prevented him from following through. Something happened to sap all his drive and determination to avenge his friend's blood—mentoring happened. Trey then took the bus home and was safe from the everlasting grip of a momentary bad decision. His friends went on to find the rival gang and ended the night in a blood-fest. Their lives were now spoiled forever; but, Trey still had a chance to do something meaningful with his life. Fatherly mentoring proved sufficient to turn around a potentially devastating incident for Trey.

But not all mentoring narratives end happily. Some end in tragedy to be sure. Ultimately, choices must be made by the mentee. And decisions are made on a moment by moment basis. At any one moment, the wise and sensible choice may be made; at another time a similar predicament may be presented but the wrong path is taken by the same individual. Where fatherly mentoring is powerful, however, is in its ties to deep-seated loyalties developed between dad and descendent. That time spent "sure-ing up" the relationship with life essentials—integrity, respect, trust, confidentiality, and security, often forges an ironclad bond. There may be constant attacks upon such well laid foundations but they will not easily crumble. During this incident, fatherly mentoring proved to be all it could be. It was enough to swing the pendulum in favor of doing the sensible thing.

Interestingly, teenage friends and gangs similarly build a deep sense of allegiance among members. So the forces Trey was up against were indeed formidable. His other friends may pressure him by virtue of the group, the unspoken but powerful code made sacred by the camaraderie. You see, we're in this together. How do you violate that sense of togetherness? That sense of "we-ism" acts like adhesive which holds gangs together and can pressure some to participate in things they would rather not partake in. Also, Trey lost a friend. He could probably hear his newly deceased buddy calling to him saying, 'Don't you care about me? Is my life worth nothing to you? Are you going to "chicken out" and let them get away with my murder?' Sure, teenage friends and gang members can cement a strong sense of loyalty too; but, there is hardly a force on earth that can penetrate the force-field formed between a loving father and his children. The special father-son code developed between Furious and Trey was stronger than the bond between Trey and his friends. But for this to take root in our children's lives, dad must wield his power in the influence of attention and get involved to cultivate and nurture a union that will be near impossible to crack.

Many sons, daughters, mothers, and fathers who participated in the *Survey of Fatherly Influence,* not only agreed overwhelmingly that it is very important for dads to "be present" and "spend time" with their children, they were equally clear about the need to "be involved" in Junior and Princess' lives and do lots of talking, coaching, building things, and going places with them. More than half of the participants recommended that father and son find a hobby to share together to help strengthen their relationship. Another 30 percent suggested that building something together would also be recommended for father and son to develop that special bond. Although the general consensus to cultivating a close connection was the same for both boys and girls, there were some clear differences among them. When it came to father and daughter strengthening their bond, more than two out of every three persons recommended that he listens to her. One standout father wrote, "Women develop ideas while speaking, listening is a show of support." That seemed to be representative of the more than sixty percent who felt listening to her was critical to father-daughter bonding. Other recommendations include going on dates with her and taking her shopping. The underlying wisdom, however, was to simply spend time listening, talking, sharing a hobby and generally paying attention to their interests and winning their confidence. These will go a long way to help deepen a wonderful father-child relationship. Another interesting feature prevalent in budding young ladies comes from the pen of Carol Gilligan (1990) who conducted research on gender differences in young people. She wrote that, "Young girls start out eager and confident, but their self-esteem slips away as they pass through adolescence." This is especially important for fathers to keep in mind since he, being male, would not intuitively relate to his daughter's teenage experiences. Parker Palmer (1998) who mentored many students, captured the essence of the legacy mentoring fathers enjoy when he said, "Mentors and apprentices are partners in an ancient human dance, and one of teaching's great rewards is the daily chance it gives us to get back on the dance floor" (p.25).

The question we have to address is how do we get involved and dance that dance with Junior and Princess? Whether it's a fast dance or slow dance, a waltz or break dance, we ought to get out on the dance floor. After his dad's passing, rhythm & blues icon Luther Vandross crooned that he would give anything to dance with his father again.

To what extent should we be involved in our kids' lives? How much is enough? What are the parameters? Here again well meaning fathers run the risk of the extremes. To some, a good father is one who protects his kids from the big, bad, world we live in and as a result they try to shelter them from all its evils. Others' idea of a good father means a more non-interfering approach—permitting Junior and Princess free reign and latitude to experience all that life has to offer with few restrictions, if any at all. These take a hands-off approach while the former group tends to be overprotective. Beginning with the overprotective method, sometimes called the sheltered approach, we may explore the terrain of father involvement.

The Sheltered Approach

"In the harbor, ships are beautiful to look at; but that is not what ships are made for." I found those words captioned beneath a beautiful painting of ships anchored to a post in the harbor. You get the picture right away; although their presence in the harbor creates a picturesque scene, ships were designed to sail the vast and turbulent oceans of the seven seas. As cargo carrying vessels, they transport people and merchandise from one part of the world to another. Whether they are cruise ships, luxury yachts, commercial cargo vessels, or sailboats they are at their best when their anchors are hoisted from the harbor and set assail. Their true purpose is fulfilled by braving the rough waves. They must get out into the ocean and navigate its currents. Of course, there is a time to dock at the harbor; such as, when they prepare the vessel for its next journey. It is at this time check-ups on the engines are conducted. Refueling, touch-ups, maintenance, repairs and readying for the journey is done. But staying fastened to the harbor signals a failure and poor use of money, time, and effort. It indicates a white flag of defeat and surrender. Some fathers lead their kids this way. Is that a healthy way to live—afraid, timid, cowering, naïve, and untested? Is that living at all? Or, isn't it merely existing?

The makers of the family movie *The Little Mermaid II: Return to the Sea* depicted this sheltered approach to raising our young when baby Melody was born to former mermaid Ariel and her human husband Eric. You'd remember that her mother Ariel was a mermaid who dreamed of life in the human world. Through a series of events she was granted her wish when she "exchanged her fins for a pair of human legs" and married Eric. Because of the evil she-monster Morgana, who wreaked havoc in the ocean, Melody's parents built a massive wall around their home to protect her from the threat Morgana posed. Like most barricades, this wall served a double purpose; it was meant to keep Morgana out but it also fenced Melody in. Ariel decided that until Morgana no longer posed a threat, the sea would be too dangerous for Melody and was therefore, off-limits to her. So she vowed to keep all knowledge of the sea from her, including her own mermaid heritage.

Young Melody grew up banned from entering the sea without any explanation as to why she was prohibited from exploring its beautiful paradise. But Ariel's well intentioned attempts at taking the overprotective route, was unsuccessful. Instead of Melody seeing this as parental love, she thought that her mother hated the sea and could not understand her natural love of it. Furthermore, by her 12th birthday, she had been sneaking out to swim in the ocean against her parents' wishes. In spite of her parents' best efforts to protect their precious little Melody, all it did was create more resentment, distrust, feelings of misunderstanding, and a sense of being unloved. It also helped develop her into a liar and a sneak. She became good at hiding stuff and living a double life.

Being anchored to the harbor of overprotective rules doesn't help Princess fulfill her true potential. Erecting walls, whether physical, mental, emotional, or psychological, usually proves more harmful than helpful. People don't fully develop when they're overly sheltered—so protected from the unsavory parts of life that they don't do much living at all. Like the mockingbirds in the opening chapter, a cagey existence is substandard and unacceptable; it's no way to live at all. A life of avoidance doesn't build into kids the skills necessary to interact intelligently, comfortably, and engage others meaningfully with contemporary world issues. Jackie Robinson, the baseball great and pioneer who helped break the color barrier in sports believed, "Life is not a spectator sport. If you're going to spend your whole life in the grandstand just watching what goes on, in my opinion you're wasting your life." Mohammad Ali, heavyweight boxing champion of the world thought, "People who are not courageous enough to take risks will accomplish nothing in life." He felt that for him to succeed at being the greatest boxer this world has ever seen required that he take some risks. Michael Jordan is not unique when he carried within him every night on the basketball court the attitude, "If you're not going to compete, I will dominate you." Sheltering does not really shelter, it stifles and paralyzes. It doesn't protect our loved ones from competing worldviews and threats to our cherished values. Sheltering may instead be fertile soil for failure. The well known proverb, "If you fail to plan; then you plan to fail," couldn't be truer when it comes to meaningfully engaging our young with a view to developing their full potential. Father ought to give attention to pressing issues; he should deal with them head-on. His involvement in his child's life requires that he face perplexing challenges. He'd do well to resist the temptation to ignore them hoping they will go away. The overprotective inclination to fathering is not good mentoring; it may in fact be a move away from coaching, teaching, apprenticing, and mentoring. What about the other side of the coin? What about lifting the overly protective shield?

The Hands-Off Approach

Some fathers believe their children should be left alone to do whatever they want. In contrast to the overprotective father, they believe their kids will find their own path. According to them, children shouldn't have any outside influences directing their lives; their own inner thoughts and drives will guide them. These fathers see themselves as mere facilitators and not influencers. Or, they may think that their greater influence lies in their ability to facilitate. They don't believe dads should infringe upon their kids' liberty to choose how to live out their lives. Any form of fatherly intrusion may be seen as tinkering with fate. They are of the opinion that children should be allowed to freely express themselves in whatever manner they desire. So they adopt the hands-off approach— a very loose, almost "anything goes" attitude toward child rearing. But the fundamental weakness with that philosophy is that children left to themselves will invariably go the way of delinquency. This kind of thinking is akin to bringing a child into the jungle and leaving her there without a map. It is not only delinquent, it is irresponsible and dangerous.

Coleridge, the English poet, once had a conversation with a man who subscribed to that school of thought. This man believed that children should not be influenced in any direction in life, until arriving at the years of discretion; they should be permitted to choose their own beliefs. At this, Coleridge said nothing except to invite his visitor to view his unkept garden where the weeds had been growing in abundance. Shocked at the condition of the garden the visitor said, "This is not a garden! There is nothing here but weeds!" Then Coleridge explained, "I did not wish to infringe upon the liberty of the garden in any way. I was just giving the garden a chance to express itself and make its own choices."

Undoubtedly, fathers ought to mentor their children; leaving them to themselves isn't an option. A garden doesn't get to be a garden without weeding, tilling, pruning, and overall care. General cultivation and maintenance is essential for the upkeep of most things. If left to itself a garden will surely be overgrown with weeds. A child's mind, heart, and behavior likewise need care, coaching, and correction. Failing to provide them the guidance and direction they need leaves them vulnerable to undesirable influences (like weeds) which will run amuck of their lives.

Both overprotective and "hands-off" fathers fall short of maximizing a positive influence in their children's lives. Without doubt, no one can rightfully accuse either of them of not loving their kids and not wanting the best for their precious offspring. Actually, it might be because of their deep affection for their adorable little ones that they have adopted their particular approach to fatherhood. The overprotective father sincerely believes he can safeguard his little princess from life's evils as well as the hands-off dad who is convinced his method gives Junior the best chance for a fulfilling life. But these two extremes have been exposed to be insufficient and flawed approaches. Neither of them is an ideal mentoring father. The overprotective dad is timid and controlling whereas the hands-off dad may be accused of being irresponsible and loose. A more balanced approach should be considered. One somewhere between the two extremes of the sheltered and hands-off approaches may prove a worthy method. Not unlike a guided tour, a method which includes a teasing out of real life encounters has a better chance of fostering maturity in Junior and Princess.

The Inoculation Approach

Before vaccines were invented, diseases like Small-Pox, Measles, and Polio threatened to inflict severe damages upon civilizations. People who contracted these diseases had little or no real defense against them. They had no way of fighting them off. They were essentially sitting ducks waiting to be shot down by the ailment. Many suffered through the course of the malady, some of whom ended up becoming permanently scarred; countless others succumbed altogether and died.

But those who successfully agonized through the disease, not only survived, but inherited an additional benefit; they built up immunity against future attacks. In those days, this "suffering through and surviving" was the only way to create protection against upcoming attacks. Survivors earned that extra benefit; their immune systems were fortified to fend off future infections before they had a chance to establish a stronghold. Special cells in the bloodstream which fought off the disease retained a memory of it. So when the virus threatened again, the immune system recognized it and launched a counterattack to prevent it from taking hold. This painful and often life-threatening process created within the individual a sort of natural immunity or vaccine against the disease.

Scientists and medical experts recognized that if they could find a way to fight off these devastating diseases without having patients suffer through them and risk death, they could save countless lives. Then the breakthrough came and the experts were able to create a way to immunize patients. Vaccines were created in a lab and could be mass-produced to inoculate millions of people. So if anyone takes the vaccine before a disease strikes, their life would be saved—the disease was declawed, it would have no effect.

Inoculation, therefore, involves injecting a virus into the body of a healthy person with the intention of fending off a threatening disease. Of course, vaccines are safe since medical experts minimize the portions used in vaccines. To the uninitiated, injecting a virus into the veins of a healthy loved-one may appear outrageous; but this practice has saved millions of lives. Vaccination creates antibodies and keeps a record of the unwelcomed imposter. This is the essence of immunity. This paradox of inoculation enables you to resist assaults from these diseases through measured exposure to them. This calculated risk protects from greater risk.

As a vaccine exposes you to the very disease it is inoculating you against and heightens your body's defenses against it, similarly dads may, **in a safe way**, carefully expose their children to some of the harsh realities prevalent in our world in order to take the sting out of them. Dad's guided exposure removes the mystery from the potentially threatening activity and its sting is nullified. This, of course, calls for a measure of wisdom and understanding. Effective dads apply wisdom in knowing what "life viruses" to expose kids to, when to expose them, and how to go about exposing them. These fathers also have the understanding that an appropriate amount of exposure will work much like a vaccine does. They understand that being either overprotective or "hands-off" will only make their children more susceptible to failure. Nowadays, dad doesn't have to expose them per se, because kids are bombarded by threatening vices on a daily basis. He needs to instill in them proper values; he needs to give them the proper perspective when thinking of threatening vices. Candidly discussing drugs, sex, violence, or any predatory life virus, in measured amounts inoculates Junior and Princess. Resisting the impulse to be overprotective or hands-off, dads may instead declaw the monsters threatening to ravish their kids' lives by telling them the truth about these ravenous beasts which won't go away simply by ignoring them. Dad would be wise to foster such a relationship with his children that they feel comfortable to discuss anything with him. This way, he has a chance to inoculate them. He will have the opportunity to shape their understanding. This is the essence of true mentoring. Both avoidance and overexposure are two extremes. The trick is to have contact without contamination.

To many, the inoculation approach may appear risky; but in fact, it is both wise and effective. The world we live in can sometimes be unkind and cold. Not everyone has Junior and Princess' best interests at heart. Keep in mind that over-protectiveness may be dangerous to Junior and Princess. Being overly-sheltered sets them up for failure. They will be left wide open to the full attacks of many "life viruses." When they finally encounter these "life monsters," and they will, they'll be clueless about how they should be dealt with. The idea is to have exposure in harmless and controlled amounts. Exposure in safe doses is an effective way to declaw life's inevitable viruses intimidating the young. This may be done by administering the jewel of the mentoring magic—casual coaching or teaching in such a way that learners are unaware they're being taught. They should just be enjoying the relationship while everyday learning is taking place. No one likes being lectured to or being singled out to be preached at. Dads may lovingly provide Junior and Princess a proper perspective on life's issues as a regular part of their interactions, mixed-in with their dialogues, humor, and overall camaraderie.

It is naïve to think that fathers can shield Junior and Princess from all the evil influences lurking behind every Facebook page and internet site waiting to ambush them? There are simply too many insincere, untrustworthy, and deceptive con-artists plotting to corrupt our unsuspecting loved ones. Neither mom nor dad can police their young twenty-four hours a day for seven days a week. Even if you could, monitoring your child's every move does not build confidence and trust in them. It isn't a healthy way to live; the young need to be allowed to breathe and make some of their own mistakes. It is better to have Junior and Princess make some mistakes when we're around so we may guide them, than for them to sneak around, make bigger mistakes, and be ashamed to face their parent.

I know this is difficult for some dads. A better approach would be to talk to them about the realities of the unsavory aspects in life rather than take the chance of having them come to their own conclusions after encountering them in a perverted manner. In my day, the bad guys sat at the back of the classroom and conducted their own version of sex education, and held strong opinions about how to deal with violence, and drug experimentation. That was neither the place nor the experts from whom to learn about those potentially dangerous vices. Nowadays, social media like Facebook and Twitter may be Junior and Princess' regular watering hole, pimp, sugar daddy, or gang leader. But there is no substitute for fathers' involvement in his kids' lives. To get maximum benefit from the influence of attention, father has to get involved and pay attention to the needs of his children. This is better done in an informal manner, in stride with the normal tempo of everyday, casual living.

The leaders at software giant Google, insist that their popular corporation maintain a family-friendly and casual feel. Their break-rooms are furnished with roundtables to encourage workers to sit next to each other to build worker relationships. They did this because they recognized that their best ideas often came from casual chats around the water coolers during break-times. Deep learning often takes place when we're relaxed and unsuspecting of "a lesson." Interestingly, Jewish fathers were instructed to mentor their children through life when they go to bed, when they rise up, when they walked by the wayside and as they talked along the way. In other words during the casualness of everyday life when they're not expecting a formal lesson, that's the time to teach them.

Furious was both present and involved in Trey's life; he didn't bury his head in the sand. He didn't simply talk about bulls; he got into the bullring, rolled up his sleeves, and enjoyed the adventure with Trey. In the casualness of everyday life, he applied the inoculation approach—carefully exposing his young son to the stark realities of life in a measured and calculated manner whereby he could coach him through them.

Unfortunately, many people's approach to fatherly mentoring is like the proverbial ostrich which buries its head in the sand. It is growing increasingly difficult to shield and protect our young from contemporary vices, traps, addictions, and snares. A wise father talks to his children (not from a distance) about these threats so he can provide them his store of wisdom and guidance. It has been said that many a false step is made by standing still. Doing nothing, when we should be proactive, only creates naïve and frightened kids who grow up ill-equipped to deal with life's challenges. There is no virtue, glory, or merit in being naïve. An ancient rhetorical question still resonates today, "How long you naïve ones, will you love naivety?" Kids should be in the know; not kept in the dark. Naivety sets up Junior and Princess for a life of victimization—accepting failure and being puzzled as to why things don't often seem to work out.

Moreover, a majority of the *Survey of Fatherly Influence* participants indicated that they do want their fathers to mentor them. They welcome dad's input into their lives. They seek advice and want to have his take on life. Children desire their father's perspective. Effective dads understand their influence of attention in their children's lives so they roll up their sleeves and get involved. They resist the urge to be over-protective and they don't leave Junior and Princess to their own devices. They apply their version of the inoculation approach enjoying an attentive involvement with their cherished offspring.

Chapter 7

Dad's Influence of Application:
Being A Role-Model

*Let every father remember that one day his son will follow his
example instead of his advice.*

—Author Unknown

The Value Of Models

When the population was expanding in Arlington,
Texas, city planners decided to build a new town to
accommodate the bulging expanse. Because these
projects incur enormous cost, a model of the new town was
setup so planners could see the finished product. This model
helped civil engineers go from abstract idea to concrete reality,
from conception to implementation. They carefully explored all
options to ensure the best possible decisions with the resources
they had. City officials, along with civil engineers deliberated
over where they thought it would be best to cut the roads, lay
down railroad tracks, zone for residential living and commercial

centers, and decided on the types of buildings that would grace the western landscape. If there was a body of water they needed to work around such as a lake, they prepared for that too.

Every year the highly competitive automobile industry is pressured to be innovative and mass-produce new and exciting cars for a demanding consumer public. Their engineers spend countless hours building and showcasing their latest model cars at auto shows around the country.

When military commanders are faced with engaging the enemy they cannot afford to overlook any possibilities and make costly mistakes. To give themselves the best chance at success, their engineers first craft a model of their strategic battle plan.

NBA, MLB, and NFL coaches sketch out strategic plays, run scrimmages, and practice religiously providing a model of game time scenarios to maximize their team's chances at success. Michael Jordan was notorious for practicing so hard, his teammates reported that "his competitiveness doesn't allow him to lose—even in practice." His "Airness" himself explained that he treats his practice sessions like real games so that during games when you don't have time to think, you just rely on instinct and muscle memory. To him practice was a model, a simulation of an actual game.

Hollywood and Broadway actors and actresses don't merely learn lines of dialogues and monologues when attempting to perfect their parts; they research the character, and role-play scenes until their performance is convincing to their audiences. They rehearse their performances over and over before opening night arrives. We know they have succeeded because they convince us to suspend disbelief and, for a short while, trick our minds into believing we are witnessing reality.

This obsession with perfecting the desired model before building the actual finished product speaks of the enormous value in providing simulation—a model. Whether they are experienced municipal planners, real estate moguls, the competitive auto industry, or the highest levels of entertainment trendsetters, they will not proceed without first seeing the finished product in a model. They understand the power of having replica so they can, in a timely manner, thwart any threats to success and have ready their absolute finest. In much the same way, fatherly mentoring provides children a real life model of how to do life. No, fathers don't model a perfect life before their kids, but they provide them opportunity to "apprentice" before opening night, before they're on their own. This apprenticeship gives them a safe place to make their mistakes. Kids get a visual showing how dad did it. Like a constant rehearsal day-after-day, youths witness first-hand how various scenarios in life are lived out. They get to see both what worked and what didn't. And they have opportunity to choose whether they'll adopt that behavior into their lives. Like the city planners, military leaders, and entertainers, the cost is too high to squander their resources. Junior and Princess' lives are ultimately at stake. You don't get a second chance at a once in a lifetime opportunity. Princess and Junior have only one life and one chance to get it right. Consciously or subconsciously, they will be looking to their parents for model behavior.

Dad's influence of application furnishes kids with an up-close and personal look at their dads. It grants them insight into adult, responsible, living. Their interactions, in many different settings and during the ordinariness of everyday life, give them a model at which to look; it's like an extended rehearsal. Over a lifetime they act out many scenes (not made-up) in the nuts and bolts of life. Kids have the chance to become experts at skillful living before they have to face life on their own, they can hone their life-skills. Dad as role model provides them one of the greatest stages for rehearsal. Did William Shakespeare understand this connection centuries ago when he wrote?

> All the world's a stage,
> And all the men and women merely players:
> They have their exits and their entrances;
> And one man in his time plays many parts.

One of the many parts a man plays is the role of father. How well he understands and plays his role will be known by how his kids turn out.

Mentoring fathers understand they are role-models to their kids. So before their kids get to the world stage, they take full advantage of the home stage. Mark Twain is credited with saying, "Few things are harder to put up with than the annoyance of a good example." A good role-model will disarm even the most stubborn children. Dad's example will live in their subconscious forever and they will eventually yield to its winning appeal.

Modeling Speaks Louder Than Lectures

Father's role-modeling supplies a three-dimensional, audiovisual answer to Princess and Junior's question: How do I do life? Or, what does skillful living look like? The influence of application satisfies the need to know how a thing works. How are all these life concepts applied to real life situations? Abstract and complex ideas are difficult to grasp especially to developing minds. We're told that the mind doesn't fully develop until around 25 years old. To make things easier to comprehend, the young need concepts to be taken out of the theoretical and placed into the practical. A model does just that. Learners don't have to imagine; they have a replica, a model to look at. Seeing how something is done as opposed to verbally explaining it clears away fog; things instantly make sense when they are modeled. More questions get answered; mysteries are solved.

Junior wants to know what you do when he tells you, "You said I shouldn't lie, but when the police asked, I denied that your fugitive brother stayed overnight because I know you didn't want them to find out." Kids don't want to know what dad says as much as they want to know what dad does. They're not listening to hear dad's skillfully contrived explanations; they're watching to see what we do. Don't tell me; show me! Contrary to popular belief, telling is not teaching. Telling Princess the same thing 100 times doesn't mean you've taught her anything. "But I told you the same thing over and over again; how many times do I have to tell you the same thing?" No effective mentoring has taken place. It may, in fact, serve as proof you're not getting through to her. Showing her, demonstrating it to her, yields better results. Sometimes you have to learn to do the thing and then teach it to them. And if they were promised consequences for violating house rules, be sure to follow through with the consequences; otherwise, you're reinforcing "dad can't be taken seriously." They're looking to see what we do.

Many fathers have failed to get their children to avoid say, smoking because they themselves are smokers. All the explanations and even warnings to Junior that "if I catch you smoking I'll @#!&$%," didn't yield the desired result—Junior still ended up with a smoking habit. Why? Because he had been receiving mixed signals from his father. On the one hand, he sees dad blowing rings of smoke in the air. On the other hand, the "old man" preached about all the sensible reasons Junior shouldn't touch the thing. When kids are faced with a dilemma like this, it is the behavior modeled before their eyes that usually wins out, not the rhetoric their fathers preach. They'd probably say something like, "I've been trying to hear what you say about not smoking, but the sight of you drawing hard on your *Camels* was drowning out your words." The maxim, "action speaks louder than words," proves true. For our kids today, modeling speaks louder than lectures.

In this chapter, we explore dad's influence of application. We extract the knowledge from dad's experiences, taking it out of dry, boring, lecture mode and inserting it into brilliant living mode by being a role model to his children. Naturally, this is easier said than done; it is easier talked than walked. But it is in the "doing" not merely the "saying" that life lessons are truly taken on board.

Dad as role-model to his kids provides them a living, visible, audible, and touchable reality that will live on in their memories. Kids will observe how dad is when things are going well and how he reacts when he's under stress. They will be aware of how he interacts with bureaucracy. They will gain valuable insights observing times he meets with the principal, and how he talks to her, etcetera. Kids will have a model of how dad drives, thinks about political candidates, thinks through difficult issues, and thinks about issues of the heart. He will display whether he knew when to speak and when to refrain from speaking. They will be able to think back to how he handled times when it might have been easy for him to take something he always wanted that wasn't his, and when he was pressured to fabricate a lie to get out of trouble. Role modeling may be the clearest evidence for skillful living a father provides his kids. It has a powerful influence in their lives. The survey respondents thought so. A majority of survey respondents believed that their father's greatest contribution to their overall sense of identity was how he lived his life. They felt that his beliefs and his character helped shape them into who they have become.

As an example to his kids, a father may intentionally model what he considers the pillars of a successful or wholesome life.

Modeling Transparency And Authenticity

Jared lives with his picture-perfect family in Staten Island, New York. He and his wife Elaine have three children, Sharon, Jaden, and Corey. One time his oldest son, Jaden, found himself between a rock and a hard place. His girlfriend informed him she was pregnant with his child. Now, Jaden's family believes children should be born to a man and woman who are married to each other and prepared for the responsibility of taking care of them. Not only was Jaden seventeen years old, in his last year of High School, and unemployed, he had the additional pressure of not being able to approach his dad with this dilemma. He feared his father would "kill" him because he would not only be bringing a strain upon the family's resources but he would also be bringing shame to the family name. His dad, who was a high school Principal, left no room for error; he set an impossibly high standard for his kids to live up to. One wonders who could ever live up to them. There were many times Jaden and his siblings resorted to running covert operations, sometimes devising elaborate schemes so they could mastermind some breathing space during their teenage years. In a panic, Jaden surveyed his options. He could finish school and get a job; when the baby is older, he could always go to college later. He and his girlfriend could elope, get married, and skip town to avoid all the family drama. He could terminate the pregnancy; no one has to know except his girlfriend and himself. Or, he could accidentally fall off the Staten-Island Ferry and all his troubles will be over. But one thing he could never do is talk to his father about it.

Pressured by the thought that he didn't have much time to decide, Jaden made the only choice he felt he could make. He spoke to his girlfriend about terminating the pregnancy and within a week the transaction was done. He was both ashamed of himself for his lack of courage and relieved that his girlfriend was willing to go along with the plan. Jaden must now live with the knowledge of his decision for the rest of his life.

Years later, Jaden spoke about the home he grew up in. Like a troubled patient on a psychiatrist's couch, he talked about the two-faced lifestyle his folks led. There was the pretty picture his family painted to outsiders. Then there were the stuffy, unreal, expectations the kids were to live up to. What made matters worse, was that his folks violated the very standards they set. One of his aunts had a habit of "talking too much" and said his father was a fraud who felt he was better than the rest of the family. His folks constantly gossiped about other family members, criticizing everything they did, and judging them for how they lived their lives. This was the confusing, hypocritical, double-standard Jaden couldn't understand. "The very things my father spoke against he did freely. He must have been blind to his own faults because he was quick to point out other people's flaws. The worst part was that dad acted like he never did anything wrong in his life. He was such a hypocrite. There was always an awkward distance between him and us."

I cannot think of a more important behavior a child may observe in a father than that of transparency. Transparent fathers live their lives without harboring or concealing secrets from his family. Unless they work for the Central Intelligence Agency (CIA) or the Federal Bureau of Investigation (FBI), fathers do well to maintain a lifestyle which showcases their lives as an open book. They don't hide things in the name of "protecting the kids" as some claim. Dads who are transparent in their dealings convey a strong sense of authenticity to their kids. And authenticity ought to be the central trait from which all decisions are made. Being authentic means being real and genuine at all times. It is being the same person when with the kids and when with extended family and friends. Authentic living will confirm in Junior and Princess' minds that their father can be trusted. This is the basis of any relationship. When we break trust or betray confidence, we poison relationships. The moment we are not true to ourselves, our every move will be tainted with deception and weakness. If father lies to cover up questionable behavior, he is first deceiving himself and second, confusing his kids with mixed messages. His children will never know the real man living inside his skin. Fudging on the truth, scheming, conniving, and manipulating, establishes dad as a fake and a coward. He's a coward because it takes courage to do the right things; instead, he whimpers under the weight of tough choices. Kids understand honest mistakes; they'll forgive weak moments; love when dad admits his errors; but they will not understand deceitful behavior from dad. Honoré de Balzac understood the supremacy of authenticity when he said, "Power is not revealed by striking hard or often, but by striking true." Fathers often fear they'll lose their control (power) if their kids see their true selves. But nothing could be more empowering both to father and child than being true, being transparent, and authentic.

Children are not unaware of their parent's ways. They study them like a scientist observing a new strain of bacteria under a microscope, as if they were on CSI investigating a crime. They are familiar with his patterns; and they notice the moment those patterns change. They pick up inconsistencies in their parents' speech and actions. Many fathers lose credibility with their children the moment kids detect a shift in their behavior. An unknown poet reminds us:

> There's a wide-eyed little fellow
> Who believes you're always right;
> And his ears are always open,
> And he watches day and night.

Dad's larger-than-life hero status evaporates; his influence is compromised when he sidesteps the truth. In the beginning Junior and Princess may be confused by dad's double life, but eventually they may adopt the same behavior because it's what was modeled to them. It's what they've come to know as the normal way to live. They will master the underhanded way to get by in life but fail to develop the proper tools for skillful living. It will be easy for them to gloss over things and take shortcuts. As a college professor, I sometimes come across students who are academically unprepared; but, the one skill these seem to master is the skill of scheming, chicanery, or "getting-over."

Modeling Via Family Customs And Traditions

A powerful message dads model to their kids is that they belong exclusively to something special; and instituting family customs sends that message. Do you remember when you entered friends' homes in your childhood neighborhood for the first time? Recall that uncanny feeling that these guys, especially if they were of a different race or from another country, were in some ways similar to your family and in other ways different? You began to understand that there are some things common among all families; and, there are other practices unique to your own family. It is those special family customs unique to a child's experience which can strengthen bonds and foster loyalty of the deepest kind. Most importantly, they infuse a deep and abiding sense of belonging. So that, when all other alliances formed among friends, teammates, classmates, or any other group to which Junior and Princess belong crumble, family traditions, like an old trusted town landmark, stand amidst the debris as a loyal and reassuring presence. They know it's going to be there; they know they can always depend on it.

Interestingly, when the nation of Israel was still in its infancy, when they were little more than a collection of families, they erected monuments to commemorate their storied journey to national maturity. They celebrated certain milestones, both physical and social, as reminders to themselves and succeeding generations. Each family customarily celebrated the yearly Passover feast to commemorate the historical Passover event. Among the instituting of other mementos, each tribe appointed a man to collect twelve boulders from the Jordan River and arranged them into a pillar to mark their successful crossing. Why? "So that when your children ask later saying, 'what do these stones mean to you' you shall say to them…" In other words, they were to create memories so that when their kids come of age, the monuments and customs would trigger a sense of curiosity in their minds. "Why do we do this every year, dad? Or, what does this mean? When did all this start? What is this really all about?" As a result, fathers had the opportunity to pass on special family secrets, traditions, and histories to their young. Not surprisingly,

Jewish families tend to have tight family units. Family members tend to enjoy a strong sense of belonging to something precious, enlightening, and liberating. They know their history and are not confused about their identity.

There are many types of customs and traditions a family may adopt, some serious and some lighthearted. A friend of mine talked tirelessly about one of their family traditions practiced each thanksgiving holiday. He spoke about a football match they'd been playing for decades. He reminisced about the hype and excitement his uncles exuded whenever they talked about what they were going to do when they all come together at the thanksgiving get-together. Last year his team, made up of his father, his brother, himself and a couple others, won; and they were going to do everything in their power to retain bragging rights. That simple football game may seem small and insignificant, but it meant a lot to the family. Jeff had that relaxed sense of focus a young man has when he's benefitted from being part of a wholesome home. He always seemed to speak magnificently about his family. He appeared to have an unexplainable, settled peace about the sonship and brotherhood he enjoyed among his immediate and extended family.

Fathers may seize the opportunity to create fun, meaningful, and engaging family traditions. Proactive dads take the initiative to topple the first domino, to get things started. They create something special for Junior and Princess. The most meaningful legacies tend to be those which are connected in some way to your family's history. Is there a family heirloom, for instance, that may be passed on?—an antique watch or jewelry, a painting, a special piece of furniture? Is there something particular to your family that Junior and Princess can look forward to at certain milestones in their lives—birthdays, graduations, sweet-sixteens, etcetera? What about professional or local sports teams, martial arts, music, or poetry? Does your family customarily support one of these as a standing tradition for a long time? Maybe an interested dad can initiate building a family quilt, creating a family recipe, tracking financial markets. Whatever it is, even if it is something really serious, make it fun without losing its significance. Some families have special rites when a baby is born, and when Junior and Princess reach puberty. (I know of a couple who collected newspapers and other relics around the year their kids were born. So that when they were old enough to appreciate it, they would have a sense of what was happening around them when they came into the world.) Other families enjoy going on yearly overseas trips, on local trips, or to the national Parks. Creating and passing on family customs have been practiced by many successful families. Conscientious mentoring dads recognize the far-reaching influence of having "something special to call our own." Whether we're aware of it or not, whether it is intentional or not, each family is known by something. The question becomes, is it something my family is proud of? Is it something that builds-up and binds us together? Mentoring dads intentionally create customs that make their families proud. These customs function like a special family brand instantly recognized and known among members. Not unlike the "Apps for success" mentioned in chapter one, these customs prove to be a great source of pride. These traditions function like magnet to keep the family together. Like timely deposits of joy, they're subliminally comforting to their minds.

Moving to New York from Trinidad could only be described as bittersweet for seventeen year old Shawn. Although he was excited at the notion of moving to a new place, it took a fair amount of time to adjust to the idea of leaving the life he knew and loved.

A quiet, intelligent sort, the thing Shawn missed most was the closeness of the family unit he took for granted. What he could never adjust to was the idea of a weakened family. As he settled and made New York his home, he grew increasingly saddened by the magnetic pull and busyness of the big city upon homes. His college Professors provided no relief with their philosophical explanations suggesting that during the industrial revolution, factories lured men away from their families to bigger cities which contributed to the breakdown of traditional family life. Shawn often likened what he was witnessing and feeling to, "viewing a scene in a bad movie where passengers on a speeding train are caught-up in their own worlds, oblivious to the impending cliff ahead." The approaching danger he envisioned was "a strained family connection" because members were scattered from a central patriarchal figurehead. After enjoying only mild success with several attempts at unifying his siblings, Shawn concluded that his best bet was to create family customs in his own family. One of the things he does is prepare exotic Trinidadian foods, usually eaten on special occasions, and invites the extended family over. He does this during the summer. He plays carefully selected calypso pieces, encourages readings from renowned Caribbean authors, and stages talent competitions among members featuring comedy, poetry readings, theatre, and musical selections. "This," he confirmed, "does two things: it anchors the family, especially the kids born here, in their cultural roots; and it helps keep members connected and current with each other."

Shawn also engages in writing a letter to his children which he gives to them on the occasion of their wedding or when they are moving out of the house. This letter, a declaration of his "absolutely essential principles from lessons learned in life," is thoughtfully prepared and delivered as a rite of passage. It is an occasion the young adults look forward to because they know it will be personal to them. They anticipate dad's matured thoughts about life to be a true treasure. A form letter outlining several categories is presented below. Of course, a father may add to or omit any category he deems important to his legacy. It might be nice to create a family letterhead as a sort of unique family brand upon which to craft this "rite-of-passage" letter.

Legacy Letter
Lessons Learned in Life
To My Son or Daughter
From Your Dad

About Them

>Tell your son or daughter how you felt about them the moment you first saw them or held them in your arms for the first time. Tell them what you noticed about their unique personalities or habits that makes them, them. Tell them how much you love them and what about them makes you proud.

About Me

>Tell your son or daughter things they may not know about you that you want them to know, things you feel may help them understand themselves or help them be successful in some way.

God

>Tell your son or daughter what you learned about God.

Family

> Tell your son or daughter what you learned about family and their place in it.

Education

> Tell your son or daughter what you learned about learning.

Work

> Tell your son or daughter what you learned about work (Job, Career, Profession, Skill, & Hobbies).

Fun

> Tell your son or daughter what you learned about fun (Leisure, Recreation, Socializing, Sports, & Hobbies).

Relationships

> Tell your son or daughter what you learned about relationships in general and particular relationships such as: Spousal, Friendships, Siblings, Family, Coworkers, and Acquaintances like Mailmen and Store Clerks, etcetera.

Possessions

> Tell your son or daughter what you learned about possessions, both material and non-material.

Modeling the ideals of family traditions conveys to Princess and Junior that they belong to an exclusive club which believes family is important. Equally significant is the additional benefit of the powerful message sent to members that their parents care about them. And it functions as a built-in chaperone by making it difficult for them to violate sacred family values. For, every exclusive club operates within certain necessary guidelines. As a member of their exclusive family club, they will want to honor its special code of ethics.

Leaving A Fine Legacy

Men have always been concerned about whether their names will live on after they're gone. This desire to leave a legacy tends to get stronger as men grow older. It becomes more and more important for us to know that our presence on planet earth left an impact on somebody. We take comfort knowing that our lives were not lived in vain. But it's one thing to know that I will be remembered; it is quite another to wonder what I will be remembered for. What kind of taste am I leaving in people's mouths about me and about my family?

Whenever a man seriously considers his call to be a role-model, he inevitably questions his qualifications for the task at hand. Many, you'll recall, received their wake-up calls the moment they cradled their tiny tots in their arms for the very first time. Like a portable fortress, he wraps his rugged arms around baby as his entire body protectively encircles her. He finds himself dutiful to the task despite a nagging notion that he is clueless about how to proceed. Dad quickly learns that in order to be a good role-model, he can no longer get away with ignoring certain habits to which he previously paid only passing attention. But he's not perfect. Like the very best of us, he will have his share of slipups. Good mentors have learned how to use even their flaws (we all have them), as a tool to pass-on authentic life lessons. That need to leave a fine legacy with our kids seems part of our DNA. But, who grades our best efforts at the end of the marking period? Who gets to decide what constitutes an "A," "B," "C," "D," or "F?" Or, whether fatherhood is graded on a pass/fail scale? One of my respected professors, who served as a mentor to me, was recently graded before a gathering in his hometown of Dallas, Texas. Knowing him as I do, I am confident he would have welcomed this discussion.

Bill Hendricks, third child of Howard Hendricks with whom he coauthored a book on mentoring, *As Iron Sharpens Iron*, spoke at his dad's memorial service in March, 2013. Following his two older siblings—who honored their beloved father with an honest, balanced, authentic, and heartfelt eulogy—Bill sought to find a fresh and unique approach to share his thoughts with the sympathetic audience. He appeared to be verbally fumbling around when he first approached the podium, but finally found his footing when he uttered the words, "Dad wasn't a great dad but he was good enough." Talk about keeping it real! I can assure you, no one in the audience thought any less of Bill or his deceased father when that sentiment was offered. But if they did, what followed was certain to remove all doubts about the character of the respected and beloved deceased. Bill went on to clarify that fatherhood is not an exact science; there are no perfect dads on the planet. All we can really hope for is a dad who is good enough.

Believing that his dad went to heaven, he imagined out loud that God put his worried father at ease about the life he modeled before his kids. In his imaginary setting, his heavenly father orally examined his earthly father. Bill thought God probably began with the words,

Well done Howard! Good and faithful servant. Enter into the joy of your heavenly father. Then He proceeded with, Howard, remember all those times you cried out to Me about your role as a father? Howard, did you love your children's mother and treat her right? (It is known, "One of the most important things a father can do for his children is to love their mother.") Knowing his father, he mimicked how he would respond. With lowered voice Howard replied,

Yes!

Did you provide for the family I gave you?

Yes!

Did you hang in there and trust Me for grace and strength when times were tough at home and did you remain with the family, instead of running away?

Yes!

Did you talk about Me? More importantly, did you have a real, evident relationship with Me that they could see?

Yes!

Did you try to instill My ways and My values into your children?

Yes!

Did you communicate to each of them that you cared how each of them would turn out?

Did you remind them that each of them had gifts that I gave them? That they mattered? And that each of them really could and should make their lives count?

Yes!

Did you celebrate their successes?

Yes!

Did you do your best to communicate to them that you love them? Even if sometimes you struggled with knowing how to express that love? Even if your expressions sometimes missed the target?

Yes!

You did all that?

Yes Lord, all that!

Howard, you were a good dad! You did all of that and more!

Now, when it comes to appraising the effectiveness of a father's influence in his children's lives, God, the giver of life, is the ultimate arbiter. Apart from God, who better to make that judgment than the kids themselves? For Bill, being a good dad was good enough. I get the feeling that their father, Howard, understood that his ultimate legacy lay in his kids. Each of them stood before witnesses and delivered a candid and fair evaluation of their less-than-perfect dad. I have since asked myself, "How will I do on examination day?" Maybe it wouldn't be a bad idea for dads to come up with a list of questions they think they'll be asked when it's time to settle accounts. I've found that these types of exercises have a way of getting us to check ourselves to see how we might be doing with our kids. Fashion a fine legacy.

Chapter 8

Summary

A man never stands as tall as when he kneels to help a child.
—Knights of Pythagoras

C hildhood experiences lay the foundation for a person's future. What happens during those formative years determine the life they eventually live. Good, bad, indifferent, troubled, confident, nervous, peaceful, or happy may largely depend upon those early years. It was that phenomenon which directed the writing of this book. An unforgettable experience in the author's life occurred when his Junior High peers boasted about weekend adventures with their dads. That standout occurrence awakened my sensitivities to a father's influence in the life of his kids and served as a major catalyst for my search for wholeness.

If the strength of a nation lies in the homes of a people and the father (the backbone of the family) is either missing or passive, then the people are heading for trouble. Although both parents are indispensible to their kids' success, the father in particular fashions a fine legacy when providing loving leadership, affirming their child's identity, being present, being involved, and being an example.

Dad's disengagement bears too heavily upon his offspring to be casually brushed aside. He is more than a sperm donor or a mere money machine: he is a kid's hero; a tour guide through the turbulent teenage years; an experienced and knowledgeable mentor; a real life example; and a protector; to name a few of his influential fatherly roles. When father understands his importance in little Junior and Princess' lives he can, with full confidence, forge ahead when providing them proper guidance.

Fathers who understand their children's personality affirm their overall sense of identity. When dads validate their kids' sense of identity, they develop confidence which enables their self-esteem to rocket sky high. These kids are able to face anything life throws at them: they will be resilient through the disappointments in life; and they will be firmly grounded and not easily carried away during life's highs. A levelheaded, sober-minded, and balanced self-image is pivotal to sound decision making. A daddy's affirmation provides kids that sense that "all is well" which gives wings to his "coming of age" young adults.

The intentional and strategic nature of mentoring transmits knowhow and empowerment to our precious upstarts. The alternative aimlessness, hit-or-miss, hopeful, trial-and-error, wishful, and circumstantial, conveys the message that dad may not care enough or may not know how to be decisive. Successful people are not known to live by happenstance; they're surefooted, steady! And fatherly mentoring includes the key ingredient of natural affection for Junior and Princess. With this combination of purposefulness and affection, a winning method is in place.

Dad's leadership method can either propel his kids to maturity and life success or it can impede their ability to thrive in this tricky world. The opposites of tyrannical and passive leadership styles experienced by many children both fail to deliver the best influential results. Those approaches aren't child-centered but father-centered. Instead, a more kid-centered method which infuses irresistible servant-leadership and balanced sensitivities is preferred. Dad's affection is a warm blanket to his kids in this otherwise cold and indifferent concrete jungle.

Dad's Influence of Association exposes the secret of his physical presence in the home. It highlights the principle that many of life's lessons are better caught than taught emphasizing the necessity of dad *being with* his children. The osmosis principle, where knowhow transfers from a place of high concentration to a place of low concentration through a semi-permeable membrane, is at work. Children who spend time around their dads pick up their habits, behaviors, values, and may adopt his life philosophy. Dad's presence is a deterrent to men who prey upon defenseless homes, instills pride and confidence in his kids, enforces respect for authority, and develops mature judgment in them.

Interestingly, nobody who took the survey indicated that riches and material things held any importance when producing great children. Instead, they overwhelmingly advised to: Look to God, be responsible, love them, be patient with them, listen to them, talk to them, spend-time with them, and be a role-model for them. Happiness does not come from the accumulation of more and more things or from a life of ease. Materialism and "me-ism" sets you up for disappointment. Making others happy and the exercise of work to utilize your creativity contributes to your happiness. So if the goal is to prepare Junior and Princess to be independent, happy, and confident to face the world, we must help them select the important things from the unimportant. We may help them to major in the majors and minor in the minors. It was tycoon, Lee Iacocca who said, "The main thing in life is to keep the main thing, the main thing."

With the *Influence of Attention* dads move from merely being physically present to rolling up their sleeves and being involved in their kids' lives. His active involvement in Junior and Princess' lives cements indestructible bonds so that outside threats may be rendered toothless. Dads avoid the temptation of being either "overprotective" or "hands-off" in their mentoring style. Instead, they employ the inoculation method whereby they use a "guided tour" approach to being involved. It is at this level of fatherly mentoring that growing kids feel most anchored to something special—his family. It is here that dads make the biggest impact upon them because he's giving more than just his money; he's giving something more precious—himself. Kids will know that he cares. Here is where he creates Monday morning stories for his kids to boast to their friends about. Here he fashions his finest legacy with them.

Dad's Influence of Application emphasized the dynamism of replica, simulation, and example which dad lives out in real time, modeled before his kids daily. Modeling speaks louder than lecturing to kids because young people are looking to see what their leaders and heroes do, not so much what they say. There is something to be said about the notion of a young person having someone to look up to who exemplifies a life they aspire to emulate. Mentoring fathers will tell you that kids watch everything you do; therefore, it is especially important to be an authentic and transparent role-model. Dads are also encouraged to institute mementos in the form of family customs and traditions as they serve to cement family members together and send the message of "belonging to something special." Leaving a fine legacy will ultimately be judged by the kids. Live in such a way that you leave no regrets and they may be proud of their dad.

Appendix

Survey of Fatherly Influence
Participants' Demographic Data

Age Distribution:

Under 18   (3)
18-29   (26)
30-39   (22)
40-49   (26)
50-59   (11)
60-69   (9)
70-79   (1)
Undecided (2)

Gender Distribution:

Male (70)
Female (30)

Parental Influence:

Raised by:
Both Parents (56)
Mother (37)
Father (2)
Surrogate Father (1)
Grandparent (6)
Aunt (2)
Sister & Bro. in Law (1)

Personal Parenting Experience:

I am a parent (62)

1. **Parents are a success when they...**
   - ☐ Provide their children the basics: food, clothing & shelter **(36)**
   - ☐ Leave an inheritance for their children **(7)**
   - ☐ Prepare their children to leave home at 18 or shortly after **(5)**
   - ☐ *Prepare their children to be independent, happy and confident to face the world (87)*
   - ☐ Other **(14)**

   - All of the above
   - Teach their children good moral values, respect for self and others
   - Teaching mutual respect and understanding
   - Spirituality and physically
   - Act as shepherds over their children: guiding, caring, protecting, disciplining
   - Educate their children: Academically, Spiritually, and Psychologically. A good education is the inheritance parents can leave.
   - Make sure they do their homework from school
   - Have given their children the tools they need to survive independently from them
   - Love their children and esteem them, set healthy boundaries and teach them about Jesus Christ
   - Love them
   - When they are role models to their children.
   - Prepare their children to be empowered to change the world
   - Provide mental and financial support
   - Provide safe, loving home

2. My favorite memory of my father was

When He was Talking/Telling Stories

- His stories about his childhood
- Being able to talk with him about anything
- Telling funny jokes
- The times when he was making jokes
- Of him telling jokes and making me laugh
- Storytelling, general occurrences of quality time
- Conversations about politics and African-American History
- His times of laughing, talking, and telling jokes

Admiring His Character

- His patience and his responsible hard work to provide for his ten kids and his devotion to my mother
- His continued example of character building in my life. Eg. His care and support for the sick, his kindness to those in need, his giving in different ways and his respect to others
- Watching him get ready for work on mornings; putting on his suits for work
- His gentlemanliness and hard working ethics
- A good man
- A man who always believe in God. God first!
- That he was a minister and he was a good man
- His personal transformation from male to father and mentor
- He was a no-nonsense man

When He Provided and Protected

- That I felt safe physically and financially whenever he was around
- Being an excellent provider and protector
- Him being a good provider
- Seeing him coming from work and telling my mom, "There's a ship out in the harbor with cargo, and he's going to take a shower, rest and wake him up at 9 pm. He went to unload the ship to make extra money for us (8 children). He came back at 5 am to brush his teeth and to go to his regular job
- Provide the family its needs at all times
- When I witnessed him almost turning into superman, by jacking a guy up for trying to kidnap me and my sister.

When He Was Teaching Me
- How he educated me and supported my mother
- When I had my math homework, he was an expert
- To show the way how I could take care of family and education
- Is his advice, his open mind and his unconditional love
- When he taught me how to cut hair
- When he took me on my first date. We went to a restaurant and he informed me of all the things a "great" man should have before marriage and the importance of respect and trust
- When we used to make trips to our village and he taught us family history
- When we went bowling and he taught me how to bowl. We then started going every week and just discussed anything

- Teaching us to cheat in board games
- He was a good teacher, role model, and caregiver
- Taking me swimming also teaching me to swim
- When he helped me reach my goal of basketball
- Him teaching me how to swim, box, and play basketball
- When I was eight (8) years old, he taught me my first pick-up to meet my childhood sweetheart

When We Were Spending Time Together
- Going to our Lake house for the summer in Shreveport, Louisiana
- He used to take my brother and I to the Playboy Club in New Jersey. It was an experience
- When he took me and my sister to a park for the day and we just spent time with him
- Taking my first train ride with him; I can still see his face right now.
- Eating seafood in Bay Ridge
- Eating dinner with him and his friends when I was age 10
- Family trips
- Travel all over the country
- Playing golf together every spring
- Taking me shopping
- Taking turns with us
- Taking care of him when he was sick
- Saturday evening drive-in movies, and Sunday evening talks around TV shows
- He's still alive, but I would say going on trips with him and the family
- Traveled to another country
- His involvement with basketball

- Him taking me to a basketball game, it was the only time I've been to a game, one of my favorite memories
- When I played basketball with him
- Running on the beach
- Holding me in his arms when I fell asleep on a bus, was about 7 or 8 years old.
- Going to church with him
- When he took us to the beach, movies and played with us
- Taking me horseback riding
- When he came home
- Wanting to go to work with him rather than going to school
- I was fifteen years old when I saw my father for the first and I was so happy
- Eating dinner and going out to the movies
- When we used to go out to have a good time
- Working side-by-side, mutual corporation is important

When He Showed His Emotions
- When he came to see me in the hospital
- One time he was angry with me but after a while he took me to an ice cream shop and bought my favorite ice cream
- His rambunctious sense of humor, brilliant orator
- His passion to get me through college
- When he was crying at my high school graduation. My father rarely cries. To see him crying out of happiness for me is a memory I will always remember
- When, I became sick in the 5th grade with a fever of about 102 degrees. He left work early, picked me up from school

and took me to the hospital. While getting out of the car on the way to the hospital, I felt weak and was about to faint, but my dad turned around and picked me up to carry me before I could hit the ground. When I became a teenager, I went through a very depressing phase of my life that caused me to be defeated mentally, physically, and spiritually, which ultimately, led to me wanting to give up. After breaking down, praying, and surrendering what I thought to be my life, the Lord miraculously took away the burden and welcomed me into His presence, then I instantly experienced a transforming of the mind and a renewing of the spirit. Jesus saved my soul!!! You may be reading this and wondering, what does this have to do with your dad. Well…at an early age, my dad performed an act of God towards me, when I was sick and felt weak, before I could faint, he caught me and carried. That's just what God does. This is and always will be one of the most impacting and memorable time of my dad.

- Probably seeing him after 10 years and seeing that I have grown so much and how he felt that I really didn't need him and he was upset that I was happy without him
- Having a stepfather, I would say, having him say he wanted to be a good friend rather than a father

No Favorite Memories
- None
- None
- None
- None
- None

- None
- No favorite memories
- I did not know my father. There were no memories conceived
- I never met my father
- Seeing him for the first time. He left when I was too young to remember. Just to see him answered questions about myself I didn't know I had
- I cannot recall
- My father died when I was two years old. I was told that he provided positive leadership. My knowledge of my father is based on what I heard my brothers and sisters say about him...

Miscellaneous
- Cooking Style
- He was a handyman
- As a facilitator during family events

3. **My father's greatest contribution to my overall sense of identity was**

☐ Biological, that's all! He was either never around or very uninvolved in my life. **(24)**

☐ *How he lived his life. His beliefs and his character shaped me into who I am. (55)*

☐ Other **(21)**

When He Affirmed/Validated Me
- Telling me that I am special, that I will be somebody. Just the essentials a great father would provide to his children
- His belief system and the idea that I could achieve anything with effort and hard work and a dream
- Teaching me to be independent

His Character/Sense Of Responsibility
- A man's responsibility to his family
- His beliefs has a great impact in my life; however, I have my own beliefs and character
- Devotion to wife and children
- My grandfather showed me that hard work pays off
- His kindness, strength, dedication to his children and family
- No nonsense
- His hard work and perseverance

His Show Of Support/Provider
- Supportive in all aspects of my growth
- Being a provider for the family
- Providing me with life lessons.
- His honesty and ability to listen and understand.

Biological But...

- Mainly biological. Although I did pick up his tinkering ability, building skills and need to be busy
- Biological and fashion sense
- My father was around but we didn't have a good relationship
- Though he did not raise me, nor was very involved, he prayed for me when I was months old and gave me over to God.
- Having an absent father allowed me to realize not to do the same as a parent.
- Rarely around as a youth, but later became more involved
- Always there physically, that's all
- He was an alcoholic and that is one thing that keeps me from drinking
- Nothing! I made/Influence myself; He contributed nothing positive
- The contribution of common sense and the city of residence

4. My father's method of leadership was...

- ☐ *Nonexistent:* He was either never around or very passive. **(28)**
- ☐ *Tyrannical:* His word was the law and no one could even ask a question **(24)**
- ☐ *Collaborative:* He included others in the decision making process **(15)**
- ☐ *Servant-leader:* He led by example, was caring, and accepted responsibility when he was wrong **(38)**
- ☐ Other **(8)**

- My father was passive
- He steps back and allows me to make mistakes in order to learn from them and improve
- Ethical

Tyrannical Plus
- Somewhat Tyrannical
- Mixed—at times tyrannical and at other times servant-leader
- While his word was the law, he always said he was here to raise, guide and advise.
- My grandfather was very tyrannical
- Definitely tyrannical; my father was wicked

5. **What do you recommend** *father and son* **do together to build a bond?**

☐ Go camping/retreat together **(20)**
☐ Build something together (model train, plane, car) **(31)**
☐ *Find a hobby to share together (58)*
☐ Other **(36)**

- All of the above
- Build plus… More important build something the child has interest in

Spend Time/Do Something Together

- Spend quality time together
- Just spend time together
- Spend quality time together every chance they get
- Spend as much time with them
- All of the above. Anytime a father spends time with his son it's an opportunity to bond
- All of the above but also should include meaningful activities with homework, church, and cultural events
- Talk, play sports, eat meals, go out together, games.
- My son and I built a roller coaster together
- Do anything together
- Do things together
- Fishing or wilderness camping
- Building provides bonding, builds confidence, develops skills
- Doing any activity together towards a goal
- I believe from the very beginning, a dad should be there for his son during his early childhood stages laying a solid foundation of love with discipline, structure, and

most importantly modeling being a positive, strong, and productive man. In my opinion, when these principles are set-up and in effect, the bond will develop over a period of time Though it'll probably never be mentioned from the son, he will never forget what his dad instilled in him

- Play games/sports with him
- Exercise
- A repeated activity that the child can identify a --, location and a spot to reminisce
- Support & Conversion, as well as some of the above

Talk/Communicate
- Walk and talk with them
- Talk to each other.
- Talk and spend time
- Talk a lot about personal accomplishments and how to go about it
- Do a lot of talking to each other
- Communicate together to impact more of their emotions
- Build a relationship that your son can come to you about any problem
- Teach son valuable life lessons for example approaching females
- Tell him it's ok to have feelings
- Have candid conversations
- Conversation

Affirm/Validate His Individuality
- Everything that he can share [that] each other likes

- Identify each other's assets and help develop each other's weaknesses into strengths
- Encourage mutual respect
- Show respect
- Prepare for life in stages
- Honestly, I love my dad but I don't like being around him—he's so negative that I prefer to stay away from him

6. **What do you recommend** *father and daughter* **do together to build a bond?**

☐ Go on dates with her **(17)**

☐ Go shopping with her **(23)**

☐ *Listen to her (80)*

☐ Other **(37)**

- All of the above but also should include meaningful activities with homework, church, and cultural events
- All of the above, But more importantly, a father should be her example of what a good man is to be.
- Everything for a father and a son above

Listen Plus

- Women develop ideas while speaking, listening is a show of support
- [Listen] This is the most important thing, hands down
- Listen, talk, care, show concern, and show strength
- Listen to each other will be better
- My dad always listens to me... even to this day, but again, it has much value because of the years of growing up around him, that's the relationship bond that we've developed. Also, I can trust my dad. That's major!!
- Both listen to her, talk to her as well as go shopping
- And have a momentous tradition
- They are more observant and they need to be listened to
- Always listen but spend time with her
- Conversation
- Enjoy each other's experiences
- The same things he would do with his sons. In addition to listening to stories and shopping for social skill building.

Daughters also need to learn practical skills from their father's like fixing a leaky faucet and working on a car engine

Talk/Teach

- Teach her about men
- Teach her how to play sports
- Talk and spend time
- Long walks and talk
- Talk
- Talk
- Talk to her about life in general and about the ways of men in particular
- Give some rules and explain men to her
- I think father and daughter should have a day where they go out to dinner, talk about life and whatever problem they both could be facing. They should really get to know each other
- Ask questions and talk to her
- Give advice when required and be firm
- Offer advice from a male perspective
- Take them out on dates, teach them how they should be treated by a man
- Protect her, letting her know that women and children are precious and need to be protected, while at the same time not letting her be afraid of everyone. He must tell her how to respect and appreciate herself, what to expect from people, and talk to her about maintaining healthy boundaries with others
- Teach her about her value as a woman

- Converse together, heart-to-heart to build a more meaningful relationship

Miscellaneous
- Protect her
- Love her
- Be a true friend
- Spend time with them
- Setting aside time on one-to-one without other siblings to do anything together will build a bond.
- Read
- Talk, play sports, eat meals, go out together, games

7. What would you most like to hear your father say to you?

- ☐ I love you **(32)**
- ☐ *I'm proud of you (63)*
- ☐ I'm sorry **(19)**
- ☐ Other **(21)**

- Pride Plus... Pride is the legacy of the son following in the father's footsteps.

Affirm My Worth
- You are precious
- All of the above
- All of the above
- All of the above
- All of the above, but more importantly, I respect you
- He has said all these
- You're really not like me, and I see you trying your best
- Because the love is so clearly evident, it probably would be to hear him say, "I'm proud of you" more often
- I would like to hear my father ask me, how am I doing?
- These days my father said to me over and over all of the above. He's 83 years and is battling several chronic diseases. Thanks dad, I love you also!
- I'm sorry, I'm racist and illiterate
- Something from the heart

Teach
- This is what you say when talking to girls; This is what basketball team you should play for; This is what you must do to be successful; This is what you say when in a fight etc. Here's some money for no reason at all

- Constructive criticism

Be Responsible
- He always said, "take care of your children."

Not Around
- Acknowledge his absence.
- Explain why he wasn't around.
- Does not apply to me since there was no involvement
- Anything! He died when I was 19 years old
- Nothing

8. **I cherish my father's principles enough to pass them on to my kids.**
   - ☐ *Agree (54)*
   - ☐ Undecided **(20)**
   - ☐ Disagree **(20)**

   - Somewhat
   - Agree 100%. Never stop talking about my father's standards to my children

Learn From His Errors
   - I would like to learn from my father's behavior [nonexistent] to become a better parent
   - I hope to avoid the mistakes my father made
   - He drank himself to death... I tell my children of my father's way so that they won't do the same things that he did
   - I will pass on the love I always wanted from my dad as well as the motherly love to my children

From My Own Experiences
   - Because of my personal experiences, I have taught my daughter to be authentic, sincere, and honest. I had to discover this for myself after a journey that even my father could not take for me or spare me
   - I will show them positive examples of parenthood and encourage them to be firm, nurturing and loving parents. Mistakes and all
   - I want to age like him
   - I will teach my son to be a great father and love his children

- And have raised my children, I tried to avoid being a tyrannical type of parent. I wanted my children to know and understand that though my decision was the final, they too had a voice and an opinion in certain cases and situations.

From Someone Else
- [I will also pass on] my Mother as well And sister too
- I will pass on my Mother's principles

9. **Due to my father's absence, I attribute certain deficiencies in my life to my lack of a male father figure**
   - ☐ Agree **(19)**
   - ☐ Undecided **(13)**
   - ☐ Disagree **(38)**

   - I wouldn't be the person I am today
   - I am not sure if things would be different if he was around or that I would want it to be. I like who I am
   - My father was around but emotionally absent. I suspect I have a tendency for the same
   - My father was periodically around because of his travels
   - He made time for me, he listened to me
   - I still managed to do well but wished I had someone to protect me
   - But I am able to stand tall and proud as a success to my mother
   - But his presence was felt; he communicated with us and provided financially for us
   - My father is not absent

10. In an ideal world, I would want my father to mentor me

- ☐ **Agree (65)**
- ☐ Undecided **(13)**
- ☐ Disagree **(6)**

- He does mentor me

11. What do you perceive your role as father to be?

Quintessential Role
- The most important role of my life
- Crucial

Provider/Supporter
- To be the backbone of the family and provide for the family
- To provide for my children to make sure that they are prepared to be productive citizens
- A provider, teacher and one who listens
- Providing for my kids, being there for them, make sure they're ok
- Provide my children with basic needs such as: food, shelter, clothing. Provide him and show him love and affection. Assure him how proud you are of his/her accomplishments.
- Protector, Provider, Counselor, Advisor, Friend
- Provider
- To provide
- Provider primarily
- To be there for the child in his/her every need
- Take care of my family and kids
- Taking care of your children, financial, teaching them the right morals and listening to them
- Be hard worker, take care of them, give them love and education
- To provide a nurturing environment, leadership, protecting and the basic needs of my kids

- To provide the necessary provisions for my children and children in general to be empowered to change and lead the world
- A father should be the provider to a family and the child and teach skills that can go on for life
- See "1" above: (Provide their children the basics: food, clothing & shelter; Prepare their children to be independent, happy and confident to face the world; Other: Provide safe, loving home)

Lead/Guide

- Leader
- Being a leader and supportive to my child
- Guide him towards a good life
- Just be there to love, guide and protect
- To be a leader as well as a listener to my children. I can teach them and learn from them as well
- To provide guidance to my children and assist them in becoming productive adults
- Leader, Teacher, Motivator, Listener, and Friend
- Leader, Teacher, Provider, Supporter… etc
- A protector/friend
- Leader and friend
- Leadership as a man; character and integrity
- As a mother/father, my role is to lead by example

Mentor/Teach

- As a mentor and a bread provider
- To teach son what to watch out for in life
- To teach my children the facts of life, put it all on the table

- To teach my kids and be there for them. To be a loving, caring, respectful person to my son and daughter
- As a single parent (female) I feel that what my father taught me before my teen years, I have given to my only child
- Informational
- Teach and be a role model to my kids
- To be a mentor to my kids
- Teacher, leader, provider
- Mentor, friend
- Mentoring, supportive
- Mentor, authoritative figure
- Parent and Teacher
- Someone who is always there for his children, someone who teaches you right from wrong
- Protector, Leader, Teacher

Role Model

- My role is to be the best father figure that I can be to my children; therefore, I may instill good values, integrity and most of all character that will show when a person meet and greet them on an individual basis
- Mentorship, Priest of my home, provider, protector, man of love and honesty, and demonstrators of integrity
- Set an example
- An example for my family
- To be available and to guide by example
- Idol, strong, brave = Hero
- A leader, lead by example.
- To listen, to love and to lead by example
- To be a very good role model

- Role Model
- A model for my children
- Mentor, Role model for my children

Spend Time
- Not a father but if I was, to spend as much time with my children as possible
- Not a father yet, but I perceive my role is to prepare my children to live a happy life

Affirm/Validate Them
- Understand what the children want to do
- Care-assistance and friend of my daughter
- Raise confident kids
- To be patient, assuming difficult circumstances and hardworking
- Not a parent as yet but my role is to protect and develop intelligent, independent youths.
- There are so many roles but a father should offer the same insights, lessons, and structural foundations as a mother would
- Love them, be there, listen
- Responsible, caring, loving, active listener, mentor, role model
- Positive and responsible and be involved in a child's life
- To be respectful to the family
- To give a different perspective that mothers can't provide
- Loving, caring, protecting, understanding, teacher
- A helper, teacher, counselor, and attraction to the love of God

Strong Dominant Personality
- To be a dominant household figure and care for his children
- Strong, in charge and caring
- Not sure

12. What's the greatest lesson you have learned from raising children?

Put God First
- To raise children to adore God first
- My greatest lesson raising children are: Be one with God in your daily dealings. Be assertive. Be fair. Be mindful of their point of view. Be direct on decision making and be a great listener.
- That children need to be grounded in the church and community that instills the core principles needed for continuous growth
- Teach children religious values and the importance of education.

Listen To Them
- That you have to listen to her needs and try to accomplish them
- To pay attention to my child's behavior and listen to them
- Take time with them, listen
- To listen, understand and love unconditionally.
- Listen
- Importance of love
- I don't know yet
- That it will take patience and lots of will power.
- Be respectful and attentive to ideas
- Always keep the lines of communication open
- As a father-to-be I can't answer that just yet but I do have 2 younger sisters. I can say the most important thing to do is to listen to your children, listen to others. Be able to

speak but more importantly, LISTEN. DON'T HEAR, LISTEN.

Be Patient With Them
- Patience
- Patience
- Patience
- Patience, communication
- Patience and Love
- Patience and communicating on the child's level, as well as, repeating lessons.
- To be patient and caring
- Patience and open communication
- Be patient and caring
- Patience and being firm
- Patience, duty & care
- Learn to have patience even when they make their own mistakes in life

Be A Role Model
- Children are very aware and they learn by what they see more in the household rather than anywhere else.
- Loving and leading by example

It's Challenging
- They are challenges that needs to be faced no matter what it takes
- That it's hard being a single parent
- The hard work that is being a father. The energy needed to spend time with them and the fears of being a bad father.

- They're expensive.
- It's not easy, you have to be a role model
- It can be challenging
- In this country, very difficult
- Be a leader
- Draw the line between being a parent and a friend
- Raising children is a life-learning responsibility
- That they want and need both parents in their lives
- To provide for them; take them on outings; be there for them
- To provide for them
- They need you to be there no matter what
- Don't have a child but my mother raising me and my sister shows she has sacrificed a lot for us and still is, but looking at what me and my sister have accomplished, she felt it was all worth it.

They Make You Happy
- They're fun
- They bring you joy. They can take stress out of your life
- They're the most precious beings
- Children can make you laugh and make you cry
- Be there for them always; social, emotional etc.
- That you have to value your time with them because they grow up so fast. You must do your best while they are young and impressionable
- You're not too old to learn from anyone
- Children are the future of the society, they must [be] part of decision making
- You have to be your kid's best friend

- Molding, modeling, takes time
- Learn to compromise, but keep standards
- Not to be judgmental
- Don't discriminate others and be yourself at all times
- That I'm my Father.
- Never take them for granted.
- Don't have children yet
- I have none
- I'm still a teen
- I can learn a lot from children
- You do not ever give them what they want, but what they need
- You never stop being their father
- Each child is an individual
- The importance of providing for them
- They'll grow up
- N/A
- N/A
- I can't think of one right now! (Sorry).

13. What advice would you offer new fathers?

Look To God

- Look to God the Father above all. Look to Jesus on how to be a man
- Seek ye first the kingdom of God and its righteousness, then all things shall be added unto you according to his purpose in Heaven.
- Pray a lot and ask God for guidance
- The best gift from God

Love Them

- To love your children and always be present in their lives
- To show all the love and support they possibly can.
- Give all the love you can to your child.
- Protect, love, support.
- To show love and to represent/support their child's future
- Kiss your children often; listen to them, be tolerant
- Love them, be there, listen, know how to read
- Live, learn, lead and love
- Love your children, role model behaviors which lead to love
- Love your kids
- Love your children and your children will love you
- To love their family as much as they can because you do not know how long you'll be with them and you shall leave them good memories.
- Respect each person as distinct individuals
- Respect your children; they will respect you
- Enjoy your home/children

Be Present

- Be present physically and emotionally. Lead by example. Don't be afraid to learn from children.
- Be there and pay attention
- Don't be absent because it can scar a child
- Stick around, they're needed
- To be present
- To be there as much as possible. Be a good mentor and provider
- Be there for your children
- Be around your kids as much as possible and stay in their lives
- To stay in your child's life regardless of the nature of the relationship you have with the mother
- Stay in their lives even if you and their mother have your own issues
- To be involved in your child's life and listen
- Just to be there for your kids. It seems that the amount of fathers who are present and active in their child's life are at a decrease.
- Always stay in their child's life no matter what. Finances and other stresses doesn't matter to children. They just want to be happy.
- To be there for your children in good times and bad times
- Be there. Support both mentally and financially

Be Involved/Spend Time

- Spend plenty of time with kids
- Spent time with your children early. "Time flies"
- Get involved in their life

- Try to be a part of children's lives
- Be involved with your children
- Get involved in your children's life and always tell them you love them
- Place a very high value on spending time with your kids. And provide a nurturing environment as well as for their basic needs
- Stay involved and tell your children you love them every day.

Be A Role Model
- Be a hero to your children
- To be a role model for their kids and be there for everything, every experience
- Be a model for the young
- Be a positive role model
- To raise their kids with their spouses
- Teach your children the right way to live and be an example for your children to follow
- Don't try to live out your own downfalls through your children let them live and experience for themselves with guidance
- Make time to connect and have down time with your child at every stage and age of their life, but most of all be a godly example to them
- Don't be a boss but be a catalyst

Listen To Them
- "Listen," respect, and advise your child
- Share, listen more to children
- Listen, pay attention, be all that you can be to your kids

- Listen to the children and talk with them more
- Listen to your kids
- Listen to your children
- Listen, respect
- It's important to listen and have an open heart with your child
- Pay attention to your children whether good or bad

Be Patient With Them
- Patience, Communication
- Patience children are children and need to laugh, don't destroy their smiles by being and "contaging" them with your misery. Enjoy their laughs
- Take time with children
- Have patience with them
- Be yourself. Be patient and ask for help anytime you need it
- Take it one day at a time. Don't disappoint your kids

Be Responsible
- Be psychologically and materially ready before having a child.
- Get ready; grow up, no more "Me"
- Be courageous, avoid laziness
- Enroll in New Father programs
- Get some help and learn from the experiences of others
- To be responsible, caring and understanding
- To support, school, God, Sports, and responsibility
- Raise your kids. Acknowledge them
- Be a man; be open-minded; listen to mama
- Always take care of your kids

- Take care of your children, don't depend on anybody; stand up to your responsibility
- Always stand up to your responsibility to your children
- To never give up
- You're bringing a new life into the world, learn to provide and protect them
- Grow up! The past life is over, enjoy the future!
- He should be more flexible in regards to giving orders
- Not a father but it's challenging and probably the best moment of your life
- Imitate the good points of your father, forgive his errors and move on
- Don't have children yet
- None, learn your own life lessons

14. Please offer any additional comments on the topic of *the father as mentor* **or** *role model* **to his children.**

Spiritual Leader/Look To God

-   Fathers should be spiritual leaders for their children. Because they are going to be responsible to some extent, if their children are not ready for the second coming of Jesus Christ
-   Fathers must seek God, be led by the Spirit and exercise patience, humility, courage so their children can see it and have a foundation for their futures.
-   A father is an example of the Most High's presence here in the world. As such, his responsibility is to live and guide as the Most High.
-   Fathers need to be strong and firm, need to lead by example and above all, have a relationship with God.
-   Don't do household jobs separate from your children. Involve and engage them to do the work with you. Ask God to make you to be the type of role model He wants you to become

Be Responsible/No Excuses

-   Being a father shouldn't be a burden but a priority
-   Fathers not being around can cause emotional distress if you're not strong.
-   Fathers need to read and learn how to be fathers and not just do it by experience. The mistakes people make as parents can scar kids. More parenting classes and coaching.
-   Never use an excuse such as the age you were when your child is born. The problems you have had at the time of

birth. Because none of those things matter nor is it the child's fault. Children get older and understand life more as they do. There is no valid excuse for being an absent parent.

- I believe the basic principles and current knowledge that exists still holds true when it is based in fundamental teachings
- As a model, fathers must be present in the home; not absent from issues leaving all to mothers who may misguide kids
- Fathers—real fathers need to be there to raise their children. It is pure joy to watch your children grow and become, educated loving adults.
- Some children grow stronger with a backbone the support of a father or has a view of the world differently with a dad involved
- A role model should be responsible, be able to provide, be supportive (positive activities) have job, spend time with kids on weekly basis.
- Be a man; stay out of trouble
- I believe responsible fathers make huge impacts on families☺

Have Character/Integrity

- When a father lies to kids, that father just digs an infinite hole in the life of his kids
- Be honest; know the value of your own self worth.
- The leader sets the pace and actions speak louder than words. If you are serious about mentoring and being a man of integrity, your children will know it. If not, they will know it.

- This is a very interesting, yet imperative survey to be read and taken. Simply because it causes a person to really dig deep and examine their emotions towards, who should be a person that has the most influence on our lives. Many of us have not had pleasant experiences with this, but others have. Fortunately, God has allowed me to be blessed with a dad who chose to stick around and cope through some difficult times. Although we often times in society see dads as negative spectacles, I think we tend to forget to honor and value the ones who are in their children's lives making differences. Even though my dad won't read this…I say kudos daddy for being the best. I am, and always will be "Daddy's little girl". One of the greatest men I know on earth… I say that with permission of the Holy Spirit. I love my daddy☺

    Also, my dad has modeled genuinely loving and being in love with my mom. This is very important and valuable for a child to observe from his/her parents. I now desire for my future husband to possess some of the same qualities my dad has shown throughout the years and even now. He has definitely set a standard for me when it comes to the type of man I want to date. Unspokenly (if that is a word), he has taught me how a man can love and stay with his woman…. and that marriage can work.

    Thanks for giving me this opportunity to have partaken in the survey, even if you didn't mean for it to reach me. I've enjoyed and hope that it can be a tremendous help for you.

- The father is the parent who builds character in his children and a sense of morality. He's the parent who tells you "I didn't feel a thing, so it can't be that bad", when you get hurt playing. The father also tells you your mother loves you, and so do you grandparents, but the rest of the world...not so much. Fathers challenge their children to see things from different perspectives. He also teaches you how to thicken your skin, to look at things analytically, and understand the consequences of your actions. I didn't learn these things from my biological father. I was blessed to learn them from my stepfather I encourage fathers to always maintain a relationship with their children if they are no longer with their mother. At that point his only concern should be his emotional, social, and moral obligation to his offspring. Never give up your children!

- Being a mentor takes determination and commitment from all parties involved in the greater good of mankind. Remember, Ethics, Excellence and Effectiveness are my ways of thoughts as an individual and a mentor.

Love and Care for Them
- I will say both, a good father will always be caring about them
- Love them
- The greatest gift to any child is a supportive, loving, and caring father
- Fathers are the first male in their daughter's life so it is imperative to show love, attention and a lot of respect
- Fathers should listen, guide and care about their children. Give excess amounts of love and compassion. Must also be firm enough to discipline when needed
- The Great Recession has made it more difficult for fathers to be the traditional bread-winners of the family,

causing tremendous stress on the family bond. Love, loyalty, communication will see the unit through.

- A happy, loving father has an easier time raising children than a father who cannot be (or is not) contented.

Be Emotionally Open

If you have an argument or disagreement with your child, do everything in your power to fix it. Swallow your pride, man up, and fix it, fast.

- I believe that a father needs to show his emotions to his children since it is important for them to see what a "human" is. Having an image of a man that is not supposed to cry or show emotions is wrong since it creates creatures with abstract feelings and not humans with sympathy, happiness and emotions

Be A Role Model/Example

- Understand the Oedipal complex, lead by example, and don't say, "When I was your age." Children have age specific problems. A 14 year boy has 14 year old problems.
- As father even when you don't think your child is watching how you act with Mom, they're taking note
- All children strongly need both parents influence (positive) in their lives especially in today's society when all other influences are destroying our children's self image.
- I think the idea to have a father as a role model is the best thing. It depends on his personality, but for me, I've never spent more than three years together. It's very important

to me to have him. They always want the best for their kids.

- Discipline in love when they are wrong. Lead by example
- Parents are to be a positive influence in their children's lives
- Every move you make, your child will never forget
- Family leader, older brother, friend.
- Treat women as you would expect your girls to be treated as well as you would expect your boys to treat their mothers as examples so they gain respect from both women and men.
- Kids will look to you for guidance. They see you as their hero. They just need reassurance, love and affirmation.
- The father is the potential first mentor usually the person the child first perceive as the authority figure. We must use it or lose it in shaping his children's character.
- Take the things you admire from your father; but be sure to model it to your kids.
- Mentoring and being a good role model does not cost a lot. Try to do things you both enjoy.

Lead/Guide
- To be firm with the child and set standards for the child
- In my opinion a father shall teach his children about life as well as what to do in certain circumstances in which most people would make a mistake and have to learn from it. It's also important to learn not to react to everything and let children learn from their mistakes
- He must help his children set a target and constantly communicate with them how to aim for it. If they falter, he

must help them to assess whether the challenge is worthy of their talents. He must help them to seize opportunity and not waste it. They must not just think, but act. As their higher self, he should be there to guide them.

- A father should be the backbone to motivate and stimulate the children

Spend Time/Be There for Them

- I recommend that fathers talk to their children. Take their children places. Spend time with them and let them know that they are wanted and loved
- Fathers should always try to be part of the child's life, not just to provide basic necessities, but also to partake in activities etc.
- Even if it doesn't work out between the parents, have a relationship with the child. Don't allow it to affect the upbringing of the child
- Be a teacher, lawyer, friend, parent to your kids at all times. Share quality time with them
- Listen to your children. And spending quality time with them is the mentoring they can have
- Always try to be around
- When a good father is in a child's life, the child will definitely feel more comfortable during their lives.
- Fathers need to spend more time with their kids. Don't just drop money off. Develop a relationship with them.
- Just being there is important whether you're a good or bad father. Your achievements and mistakes will provide a learning lesson to your child. They will learn what to and what not to do from you.

- Be present, think and listen. Children needs both parents
- I'm seeing less and less fathers being there for their children, especially in the black community, I hope that changes. Children need their dads in their life.

Talk/Communicate
- Give his childhood experiences, talk about everything
- Fathers need to communicate more to their kids. Moreover they need to show more responsibility towards their children
- Be loving but be stern when it's needed. Let them know why you do what you do. They will respect and appreciate it later in life.

Promote Their Unique Identity
- Learn to figure out who your kids are, and accept them for who they are, whether or not they fit your expectations
- Be yourself so your children can do the same

Opportunity For Fathers To Learn
- Don't think of being a father as a task but rather as one role achieved in life and you can learn more at this point in time than any other point in your life
- It's a wonderful opportunity to learn more about oneself, and who their child is

- Don't forget to include the importance of step-fathers and how other men are able to step up.

- A father should develop patience within himself so he can share his wisdom with his kids—because it takes patience.
- At all times, keep a watchful eye on them.

References

Albom, M. (1997). *Tuesdays With Morrie*. New York: Doubleday.

Bombeck, E. (1988). *Family—The Tie that Binds... and Gag!* New York: Fawcett Books.

Children's Defense Fund (2012) Children in New York. Washington: DC. www.childrendefensefund.org retrieved 09/12/12.

Downing, S. (2011). *On Course: Strategies For Creating Success In College And In Life*. Boston: Wadsworth, Cengage Learning.

Gray, A. (1996). *Stories For The Heart*. Oregon: Multnomah Books.

Gibbs, N. "What Kids (Really) Need." *TIME*: April 30, 2001, 48-49.

Gilligan, C. (1990). *Making Connections: The Relational Worlds of Adolescent Girls At Emma Willard School*. Cambridge MA: Harvard University Press.

Hendricks, H., & Phillips, B. (1997). *Values And Virtues*. Sisters, OR: Multnomah Books.

Hendricks, H. & Hendricks W., (2000). *As Iron Sharpens Iron*, Chicago: Moody.

Hewett, J. S. Ed. (1988). *Illustrations Unlimited: A Topical Collection of Hundreds of Quotations, & Humor for Speakers, Writers, Pastors, and Teachers*. Wheaton, IL: Tyndale House Publishers, Inc.

LeBoeuf, M. (1989). *How to Win Customers and Keep Them for Life*. New York: Berkley Books.

Macionis, J. (2010). *Sociology*. 13th edition. New York: Prentice Hall

National Center for Health Statistics (2009), Retrieved 04/07/12 http://www.childstats.gov/americaschildren/famsoc2.asp #n4

Parachin, V. (2010). *Vibrant Life*. Cultivating The Fine Art of Good Fathering Retrieved 08/02/12 http://www.vibrantlife.com/?p=169

Palmer, P. (1998) *The Courage To Teach: Exploring The Inner Landscape Of A Teacher's Life*. San Francisco: Jossey Bass

Stenson, J. (2012). *How Does a Father Protect His Family*. Retrieved 08/17/2012 from www.parentleadership.com

Swindoll, C. R. (1998). *The Tale Of The Tardy Oxcart: And 1,501 Other Stories*. Nashville: Word.

Thomas, C. (1985). *Liberals for Lunch*. Illinois: Crossway Books.

Thomas, D. A. (2001). *The Truth About Mentoring Minorities: Race Matters*. Harvard Business Review, April 2001, p. 107.

U.S. Census Bureau (2010) Retrieved 04/07/12 http://www. childstats.gov/americaschildren/famsoc1.asp

US D.H.H.S. news release, March 26, 1999. Retrieved 04/07/12 http://fatherhoodfactor.com/statistics

CPSIA information can be obtained at www.ICGtesting.com
Printed in the USA
BVOW042017050613

322557BV00001B/27/P